Western Washington *Reflections*

Western Washington Reflections

Stories *from the* Puget Sound to Vancouver

~ Edited by ~
Rebecca Helm Beardsall & Colleen Lutz Clemens

Charleston | London
THE
History
PRESS

Published by The History Press
Charleston, SC 29403
www.historypress.net

Copyright © 2013 by Rebecca Helm Beardsall and Colleen Lutz Clemens
All rights reserved

Cover photography courtesy Brandon Sawaya. *Front cover:* Moclips, WA. *Back cover, top to bottom:* Tacoma, WA; Seattle, WA; Anacortes, WA.

First published 2013

Manufactured in the United States

ISBN 978.1.60949.852.8

Library of Congress CIP data applied for.

For Jet, Nova and Ev
May their lives bring more stories

Contents

Acknowledgements

We are both thankful for our parents—Robert and Marilyn Helm and Sandra and Barry Lutz—for raising us in the tradition of the Pennsylvania German community, which cultivated our work ethic, for without it we would have given up long ago.

We appreciate the honesty, patience and talent evident in all of the writers who generously shared their memories and stories of Western Washington. Reflecting on the past is never an easy task, and we are grateful that they were willing to take that journey with us.

We would like to thank our editors at The History Press: Aubrie Koenig for her excitement and enthusiasm in this Western Washington project, and Hannah Cassilly for believing in our project of collected stories.

Finally, we would like to thank our partners, Matthew Clemens and Geoffrey Beardsall, for listening to book talk. Without your relentless support, this book would not exist. And a special thank you to Evalaine Lutz Clemens for making our world much more interesting.

Introduction

O ver five million people lived in Western Washington as of 2010. They spread out over twenty-five thousand square miles. Some of them live along the Puget Sound, where they can watch the fins of orcas breaking the deep blue waters. Others live tucked in along the foothills of the Cascades. All fall asleep to the sound of raindrops drumming on the roofs during the winter and spring. Everyone looks to the mountains in awe and inspiration.

Western Washington is known for its natural beauty. The Cascades create the backdrop, and the Puget Sound sits center stage in a world regularly washed clean by rain. The pioneer spirit, which brought many to a land of trees larger than houses and wilderness so untame, continues in many of the transplants who now call Washington home. Western Washington is more than just nature—it is part of our lives. It is our relationship with the towns, cities and farmland that grounds us and provides the support for our livelihoods. Our lives have been shaped by the values, cultures and traditions established in this Evergreen State. Coming to an understanding of our sense of place is important to how we view ourselves. This collection of creative nonfiction about the land, people, towns and cities of Western Washington was created for us to remember our history and heritage and to honor our present-day lives and accomplishments.

In 2005, we began a journey in Pennsylvania when we took on the challenge to show our home state through the eyes of some of the state's best nonfiction essay writers. As two lifetime residents of Pennsylvania, we are proud to have edited two works that reflect the beauty, work ethic and tradition we see in the Keystone State: *Philadelphia Reflections: Memories of the Keystone State* and *Western Pennsylvania Reflections: Stories from the Alleghenies to Lake Erie*. In 2011, our lives changed when Rebecca moved to Washington. In an effort to cope with the loss of seeing each other every day, we decided another project would keep us connected. As Rebecca listened to the stories of the people around her in her new community, she realized there was a richness and depth to everyone's story and, with Colleen's help, decided to once again bring those stories to light in a collection.

We wanted to hear the stories from these thousands of square miles, the stories that come up from out of the ground of the mines and from the mountaintops, from the city streets and the lush evergreen forest, from the backyards and the trails. We invite you to share in stories from the state, linger in the spaces you find comfortable and learn something new about your neighbors who live on a different square mile. Let this book serve as a forest of stories that holds all of us—residents and transplants alike—together.

The Smith Road Chronicles

LYNDEN

By Sarah Eden Wallace

W ho's your mother?" That's how people in Lynden figure out who you are. Not where you work or what college you went to, but whether your mom was a Bonsen or a Shumway or a Van Weerdhuizen. Because then they'll know to ask if your grandparents were the Plagermans who lived off the Badger Road or the ones who lived on Front Street. No, you can explain, that's your dad's cousin from Custer who married a Zender, and that'll unleash a gusher of information about where you probably went to grade school—Ebeneezer or Lynden Christian—and whether your family raised Holsteins or Guernseys with maybe some Charolais thrown in the mix and whether you're related through the Zylstra side or were in glee club with one another's cousins and it clarifies a whole lot and moves the conversation a hunk down the road.

When I first began interviewing folks for a book, they usually asked, with a puzzled tilt of the head, "So, who are you?" I found it didn't help if I relayed that I was a journalist and former editor for what I thought was a pretty big-deal major metropolitan daily. For the first time in my life, that fact carried no weight, inconsequential as the plastic binding snipped off a straw bale. In fact, it only added to the confusion and left them with a polite glazed look on their faces. Instead, I learned to explain, "My family's from eastern Washington. My mom grew up in Metaline Falls. No one's ever heard of it; it's a small mining town about fifteen miles south of Canada." Then and only then, that unease would drop, assuaged that I slid into a slot in the universe that makes sense, and we could proceed. Oh, she's from *eastern* Washington, no wonder. I could explain that I was writing a book

For more than one hundred years, the Northwest Washington Fair, shown here in 1955, has been a way of life in Whatcom County.

about the 100th anniversary of our fair. "Oh, it's for the fair," they'd say, further relieved. "We love the fair."

Indeed they do. In most parts of Whatcom County, the Northwest Washington Fair is a way of life, not an event. "We have five seasons here: spring, summer, winter, fall and fair," says Gary Vis, grandson of Dutch immigrants and executive director of the Lynden Chamber of Commerce. He grew up on a four-acre parcel between Lynden and the Canadian border, "one of the greatest places to be a kid, ever." For people who came here from California or New Jersey or Bellevue, not so much, and therein lies a tale.

———◦•✦•◦———

Many here don't realize they live on a divide. Not in the earthquake-preparedness sense, but more in regard to what sometimes yawns into a chasm over cultural matters such as manure odors, watershed management or how many days you go to the fair. What some call the Smith Road Divide is less geography and more half-joking shorthand for town and gown: Bellingham's hilly mill town turned university town snugged into a county based on ag and making a decent living from natural resources like catching coho and cutting down Doug fir. Between these two realms, there's an expanse of field and farm that levels out north of the Walmart on the Guide Meridian. It's sliced in neat cake layers of county-line roads that run to the horizon, dipping over hills but mostly stretching in straight fifty-mile-per-hour spans by small houses, barns, pasturage, hay rolls and herds of Holsteins. About halfway up, north of the mall and south of Wiser Lake, there's the Smith Road, our vertex between urban and rural, John Deere and Subaru Outback, Dansko clogs and Georgia Romeo boots.

Sometimes, it shapes up as two ways to look at what's in front of you.

For example, at the fair, there's an event called mutton bustin'. Little 'uns in helmets and cowboy boots grab handfuls of a two-hundred-pound unsheared ewe and ride it across the freshly tilled dirt of the grandstand arena as far and fast as they can. Usually within a few yards, they slide sideways and then tumble in the soft track. The sheep jog toward a waiting horse trailer, and the crowd oohs and calls in enthusiastic sympathy. Where some on the south side of the Smith Road view mutton bustin' as "shouldn't there be a law" child and animal abuse of the first degree, others see kids learning to get back on when you're bucked off and doing your best and holding on through the tough parts when the eyes of your hometown and your people are on you, supporting you, cheering, hollering to hang on, buddy, hang on! Which is what showing livestock is all about, and farming, for that matter, and life, if you get right down to it.

That's a singular way of seeing the world. Loren VanderYacht, who grew up in Lynden and has been the backstage superintendent for the fair since 2003, often picks up at the airport the celebrity entertainers who perform at the fair. This means an hour or so in the car with the likes of Brad Paisley, Ted Nugent, Glen Campbell, Emmylou Harris, Trace Adkins or Willie Nelson. "You don't want to be star struck," VanderYacht says. "The way I handle it, if I'm driving or if we're sitting, I make it a rule I don't initiate the conversation. If they want to talk to me, they'll say something."

So he takes them up the heart of the Smith Road Divide. "One thing I try to do, if we're coming from Bellingham, I'll try to take the Hannegan (Road) up so they can see Lynden," he says. "Once they start talking about how neat and clean it is, I'll explain about the Sunday closures and all the churches and the Christian Reform. They get a chuckle out of it.

Northwest Washington Fair mutton bustin' 2009. Mutton bustin' gives youngsters a taste of livestock competition at the Northwest Washington Fair. *Courtesy of Mike Urban.*

"Lynden's just different than most places they go to. I get the feeling they'll remember this spot. I'm sure everywhere else they go seems like the last place they were at."

❧

Back in the day, everyone had dynamite. When the fair was first built in 1911, the fairgrounds had to be cleared of timber "thick as the hair of a dog," according to Luke Ferrell, who first went to the fair in the 1920s. So after felling trees the diameter of a barn door, farmers had to pry out roots that reached into stubborn soil. It took a team of eighteen-hand draft horses, double-headed axes and a shed stash of explosives.

There's a photo in the stairwell up to the photo archives of our Whatcom Museum that shows a man and a horse harnessed to a narrow wagon paused on a plank road. The label explains it's what was then and still is—in an asphalt version—the Guide Meridian. It's now our major commercial artery, lined with gas station–carwash combos and Rite Aid and Burger King and appliance stores and all-you-can-eat buffets.

That photo shows that before there was the Smith Road Divide, we were all on one road: a rough path paved with oak from our forests, hand-built by our neighbors, heading home to a farm with a two-holer outhouse, firewood to be split for the kitchen stove and water to be carried if the dishes were going to get washed. That man holding the reins in the photo is taking a break from the day-by-day hand-over-fist pull to make a farm out of a forest. He and his fellows' determination would produce alfalfa and corn and berries that are shipped to the far corners of the world and stirred into Dannon yogurt and Smucker's jam, seed potatoes that sprout into McDonald's French fries on all the continents.

When work was that hard and when everyone was broke ("We were all poor, we just didn't know we were poor," says Violet "Vi" Weidkamp, remembering her 1940s childhood), it elevated a celebration like the Northwest Washington Fair to extraordinary. It shone as the highlight of the year, decade after decade.

In that sense, the Smith Road Divide comes down to frequency. Either you immerse in all six days of the fair (never held on a Sunday in 102 years), or you dip in for a day. That's incomprehensible if you're from north-of-the-Smith-Road stock. "It was the shock of my life when I got married and

Northwest Washington Fair poster 1980.

met people who don't go to every day of the fair all day and night," says Joanne VanderYacht. A third-generation Whatcom County–ite (and Loren VanderYacht's aunt) with "sawdust in my veins," she grew up going to the fair, worked in the fair office and plans to go to the fair until she dies.

"I thought the fair was that important to everybody," says VanderYacht, now a spry grandmother. "I went to the fair every day every year of my life, except for one or two years when I was working in Seattle. It was a part of most people's lives in those days."

A divide can also be defined as a watershed, a crucially important factor, time or event—which makes me think of food.

There's this dizzying array of delights at the fair, from prize-winning pies, the Dutch griddled pastry *poffertjes* ("little pillows") and the Dairywomen's famed Moo-Wiches to corndogs, deep-fried Oreos and curly fries. To this day, Joanne VanderYacht can inhale heady childhood memories of the scent of sawdust, hamburgers and grilled onions at the fair.

But for me, one meal says what our fair is all about. It's a dinner that money can't buy; not one of the quarter-million people who now go to the fair every year can partake.

Every summer for nearly twenty years, a group of church volunteers with the tongue-in-cheek name of the Fairisees has served dinner to the carnies. As the workers roll in, hours from striking the Skagit County Fair, they face a night of torquing bolts on the Tilt-A-Whirl and testing rides for the next morning's opening. With grease up to their elbows and smudged faces, clusters of five or six unload gear, hoist rails, fire up generators and assemble canopies.

But for a half hour in the scent of fresh-mown grass, they sit at the white-painted picnic tables next to the Lynden High School PTA booth and eat.

As the sun sets on that August evening, the Fairisees grill burgers, dish out curly pasta salad and coleslaw, boil fresh corn donated by local farmers and hand out a cheery greeting along with rolls provided by the Lynden Dutch Bakery a few blocks away on Front Street. To top it off, they cut into homemade pies topped with ice cream courtesy of the Edaleen Dairy and cows the carnies probably saw on the drive up.

"They're a special bunch of people. They have very diverse backgrounds, some highly educated, some well-to-do," explains volunteer coordinator

Doug Traina. "Some your heart just breaks with them in terms of where they've come from."

After dinner, the clang of hammers and wrenches resumes. The carnival workers will work another six hours or so to set up the rides. It'll be near dawn by the time they rest.

"They say Lynden stands out when they talk about the circuit," says Traina. "It's something that they really look forward to, and it's grown up as a tradition."

Home cooking like that is much heralded in gourmet magazines and bistro menus these days, but it's what I grew up with and ate every day. It's what my eastern Washington mother learned from her immigrant mother and taught to me. I was raised with the governing principle that there's no sense buying stuff at the store if you can make it yourself and doubtless do it better: bread, pickles, spaghetti sauce, salad dressing, jam, applesauce—you name it, we preserved or caught or grew or picked or froze it. I didn't taste a Chips Ahoy cookie until I was in college.

A few years ago, my husband and I went to a Fourth of July picnic out in Ferndale, way north of the Smith Road near Wiser Lake. I'd spent the morning making a run out to Boxx Berry Farms, picking buckets of strawberries and then putting up seven batches of freezer jam. The red juice stained my hands no matter how I scrubbed, and my nails were dark-rimmed from hulling stems. Sitting on a blanket, waiting for the teens to set off the fireworks down by the pond, I was dumbfounded when Kim Bowthorpe saw the hands I was tempted to keep hidden in my pockets and asked right off, "Oh, did you make jam today?" That's a mid-summer matter of course north of the Smith Road Divide.

So we chatted about putting up jelly and the rhubarb chutney I'd tried in May and could I send her the recipe. We went over which u-pick had raspberries yet and whether blueberries might be late this year because the spring rains were so heavy. We talked about how we hate to pick blackberries with all the stickers, but it was so worth it to have the jam at Thanksgiving dinner.

During the grandstand shows at the fair, you'll find Toni Blakely helping out Rick Hollemon in the announcer's booth. Her grandfather was Harold Weidkamp, one of the first generation of draft horse drivers to compete at the fair in the 1940s.

Shaye Brandsma of Lynden leads a Belgian draft horse during junior showmanship at the 2009 Northwest Washington Fair. Her family has shown draft horses at the fair for four generations. *Courtesy of Mike Urban.*

Toni remembers busy weeks as a kid while the family showed horses. It was the job of the Weidkamp grandkids to snap bushels of green beans in the horse barn tack room. Then, each night, their grandmother Sina Weidkamp would take the beans home and can them, preparing for the long winter to come. It probably left her all of four hours' sleep each night, but like a plank road, those canned goods said we're safe, if nothing else we'll eat, we're going to make it home.

———◆••••◆———

The best thing you learn at the fair is that there's no Smith Road Divide when it comes to surviving tough times. Deep in the bones of the fair is the endurance to rise from a steep fall, whether you've been pitched off a stubborn sheep in the mutton bustin' or you're a dairy farmer buckling under rising feed prices.

Harry Bowen served as 4-H horse superintendent at the fair for twenty-four years. In 2001, his wife, Ginny—short for Virginia—had cancer. He didn't want to go to the fair because "it'll look like I'm not taking care of you."

Ginny leveled a stern gaze at Harry and declared, "You've never been able to stop me from doing something I want to do, so let's not start now. I want to be at the fair." Friends rented her a motorized scooter and hooked up her oxygen tank. She went about as always, encouraging the first-timers, visiting with the kids, cooing over the grown girls who come back every year with daughters of their own and coaching the 4-H riders. "This was Ginny and my's philosophy," declares Harry. "4-H is not about ribbons and trophies. 4-H is about raising blue-ribbon citizens. The horse or the cow or the sewing machine, those are just tools to do that."

Finally, on Friday of fair week, she said, "Take me to the hospital; I have to get some sleep."

"She died the day after the fair," on August 19, 2001, says Harry, after doing what she loved to do and had done for more than a quarter century. Four hundred people came to her funeral.

From south of Smith Road, the fair looks to be all neon rides, squealing girls, has-been rock shows, cotton candy and deep-fried everything. But when a celebration has been held by thousands of people for more than one hundred years, it takes on a greater vigor. Maybe that's why Ginny Bowen knew she needed to be at the fair in her dying days. She didn't leave this earth until her duties felt done. Then, she saw the assurance of things hoped for in the future and endless memories of a past where much seemed possible, and there is no divide, if we all pitch in.

The Rock

BELLINGHAM

By Cindy Sherwin

Years ago, when I was married and had three small children, my husband and I became anxious about living in Los Angeles and considered leaving the area. It was feeling crowded and smoggy, as well as a dangerous place to be. The riots after the Rodney King incident came within blocks of our home. We watched in horror as news programs flashed images of storefront windows smashed in and police cars overturned.

Traffic was horrid, and there was never a time of day that the freeway was not bumper-to-bumper. There were times when I would get so frustrated sitting in stop-and-go traffic that I would get off the freeway and try to make my way home on surface streets. That was always a mistake. Our family longed for a less crowded, healthier, safer place to be.

We knew Western Washington was a beautiful part of the country with a mild climate. My husband spent summers with his grandparents in Seattle as a child and often talked about wanting to live there. I visited my sister and her family in Bellingham several times before I was married.

One of those visits was over the Fourth of July holiday. Living in Southern California, I made the mistaken assumption that a visit to Washington in July would mean shorts and tank tops. My sister's neighborhood had a block party that weekend, complete with food, drink, kids, bikes and fireworks. The day started warm, but by the time we were getting ready for hot dogs, barbecues were rolled under eaves as we sought shelter from the rainstorm. Hot dogs taste just as good from inside a neighbor's garage.

So we made the decision to move to Washington and started looking for just the right place. We traveled up the I-5 corridor, checking out towns along the way. We looked at Lynnwood, Renton, Everett and other areas. We checked out real estate prices, traffic, shopping and theaters, but every place we looked felt just like L.A. Prices were high, stores crowded and the traffic awful. The farther north we traveled, the more we liked the towns we came across. There were more parks and open space and fewer malls. Traffic was lighter as the freeway narrowed to two lanes in each direction. There were beautiful hills and expansive valleys with miles of farmland. Eventually, when we could almost go no farther north without hitting Canada, we found ourselves in Bellingham.

We moved there in May, nearly twenty years ago, and never looked back. It happened to be one of the drier, sunnier springs. The cottonwoods came into full bloom shortly after our arrival. Many people around here hate that two-week period because of the havoc it plays on their allergies. I thought the nature display fun to watch. The tall trees shed their little fluffy white seed bunches, which are carried off in every breeze. In our yard, I held my one-year-old in my arms, and we made a game of trying to catch the imitation snowflakes as they floated by. Every May when the cottonwoods bloom, I remember that time.

We moved into an instant neighborhood, just add people and stir. It was a new street, and because people who moved there were from everywhere but Bellingham, they were eager to make new friends. Our house was one of five that was built and occupied; the rest were empty lots or homes in various stages of construction. A family from Vancouver, Washington, with three children moved in a few weeks before us. We had a realtor in common, so he introduced us to Tim and Brenda and their three active boys. After we lived there for a couple weeks, Brenda confessed to me that she baked us a plate of welcome-to-the-neighborhood cookies, but they were all eaten before she could get them to us.

Brenda and I became fast friends as our families grew close. We often went camping or barbecued in the backyard together, and she and Tim tried unsuccessfully to teach us pinochle. We walked the kids to school together down the trails just behind our street. The kids played together and got muddy in the creek that ran across the back of our property. But one of the most significant events in our relationship is that Brenda is the one who introduced me to the iced mocha, for which I am forever grateful.

Because we were each at home with three kids, me as a stay-at-home mom and Brenda with a home-based business, we found comfort and support in each other's company. I'm an extrovert and need adult company to recharge. With two kids in school and one home with me during the day, there were times when I went a little stir-crazy and needed to talk with someone about something other than Elmo and the letter "R." On days like that, I would meander down the street and find myself in Brenda's garage.

Tim and Brenda had turned half of their garage into a workshop for Brenda's business. She made magic with fabric, constructing beautiful window coverings and gorgeous duvets and pillows. Her workshop served double duty as a workspace for her and a refuge for me. She was so generous with her time and her attention. I dropped in any time to talk or unload, and she always welcomed me, no matter how busy she was. I pulled up a stool at her worktable as she pinned and stitched and I released my troubles, which were nearly all superficial. Most of the time, I just needed to share with someone. The kids were driving me crazy, my husband was driving me crazy, my house was a mess and I couldn't get anyone to pick up after themselves.

Brenda listened patiently and, like a good friend, agreed with everything I said and usually made me laugh. Then I listened to her, with many of the same complaints on her end. She told me about the mischief her boys had gotten into or how hard it was that her husband worked such long hours.

A few years later, the tone of our conversations changed suddenly. I confided in her the horrible suspicions I had about my husband, who was spending too much time with another female friend of mine. One evening I caught him lying to me about something trivial, involving the friend. He stumbled and muttered and finally admitted that he was unhappy in our marriage but for a long time denied the fact that he and my friend were indeed having an affair. He pretended to try to work it out with me, even going to a marriage counselor. But a marriage can only work when there are two people involved, and ours had three. Eight months later, he moved out, still denying the affair.

Brenda became my lifeline. I called at any hour, and she was there for me. I remember countless days during those eight months, with me sitting on the floor, leaning against the bed in the guestroom with the door closed, crying, on the phone with Brenda. Every new thing that happened that pointed to him being guilty was like a knife ripping into my heart, and I shared my pain with her. She stayed on the phone with me almost daily, sometimes for an hour or two, listening and comforting, trying to help me understand what was happening in my life and how it was affecting my children. My husband had always been my best friend in the world, and I trusted him more than anyone. But I could no longer turn to him for comfort or support.

Within days of my husband moving out that December, Brenda showed up at my door with a large wicker basket full of love. She brought new sheets for my bed, bubble bath, candles, fresh flowers, a book of inspirational quotes and, of course, chocolate.

Time moved on, and I moved on. Our neighborhood grew, and more families moved in. We watched each other's kids, had block parties together and organized neighborhood cleanup days. Coming from a city of eight million people, I am enamored with living in such a small community. The fact that so many neighbors get so involved with one another is contrary to any experience I'd had in California. But it's not just about the neighborhood: it goes beyond that.

There are many facets to living in the Northwest, and when it comes to celebrating events, there are many choices built in to our corner of the world. Vows are renewed on the beach at Larrabee Park. Family reunions take place at the Hovander Homestead or the campground at Birch Bay. Weddings are celebrated at Lairmont Manor and birthdays at the park at Lake Whatcom. Senior pictures are taken on the boardwalk at Boulevard Park. Memorial services are performed on the bow of a boat cruising Puget Sound. But one of the most unique ways to commemorate just about any occasion involves the Rock.

It's on a stretch of road just south of Bellingham where two lanes of freeway wind through and around woods and mountains and lakes. It's such a beautiful strip of road that it still takes my breath away, even after living here for nearly twenty years.

The woods along that stretch are so pristine and untouched that it's hard to imagine as you're driving along that there's a fairly medium-sized town just ahead, around the bend. Alongside the northbound lanes is the Rock. It stands probably fifteen feet tall and is as wide as a car is long.

Sometimes it expresses birthday wishes, sometimes welcome home messages. In May and June, various graduation acknowledgements can be counted on, changing almost daily. Everyone living in Bellingham or in any of the small communities between Bellingham and the Canadian border knows about the Rock.

I don't know when the tradition surrounding the Rock started, but I'm guessing it goes back to when paint was first invented. There are so many layers of paint that it sticks out two feet or more. Some say that the Rock, for which you need a ladder to reach the top, is actually a mere pebble that has been painted so many times over the years that it has grown to its present size.

It only takes a mention of it among a group of neighbors or at a Bunko party, and someone will have a story to share. The one time in my life that I got to participate in the ancient tradition was to celebrate a special anniversary.

Tim and Brenda were about to celebrate their twentieth wedding anniversary and wanted to do something big to mark the occasion. What could be a more resplendent expression of love and commitment than painting a giant rock alongside the northbound lanes of the interstate highway?

There is no easy way to get to it. When Brenda and Tim researched it, they found that there is nowhere to park nearby in the woods behind it and walk in. There are no paths leading to it. There are fences and other obstructions that make it impossible to get to. The only way to get to it is by parking on the shoulder of the highway next to it.

I'm pretty sure it's illegal to park on the shoulder of I-5 unless in an emergency. Emergencies that would qualify would probably include a flat tire, a falling rock breaking through your windshield or an engine fire. I'm almost certain that painting the Rock does not qualify. However, I am astounded by this fact: in the nearly twenty years I've lived in Bellingham, the Rock has probably been painted more than 5,000 times (that's 250 times a year, probably a conservative estimate), and not once have I ever heard of anyone being ticketed, towed, harassed or arrested for parking on the shoulder alongside the Rock.

The afternoon of the anniversary began with a backyard barbecue party, where family and friends of the couple gathered to celebrate. It was an unusual June day, in that it wasn't raining. I introduced Steve, the man who would later become my husband, to my co-conspirators. There was excitement all around with clandestine discussions about rock painting plans. Supplies had been gathered, research completed, logistics determined and giant heart-shaped stencils constructed. Steve, a painting contractor, contributed ladders, brushes and rollers.

After the barbecued ribs and coleslaw were consumed, we divided up into a convoy of three vehicles. With Tim and Brenda in the lead, we caravanned to the site. We unloaded the equipment, which included about twenty cans of spray paint. The project began by diligently covering up the most recent salutation with a coat of white spray paint, acting as a base for the pink hearts. We acted quickly and efficiently, except, of course, stopping to take pictures of each friend and family member holding a spray can or a roller, posing in front of the Rock, mid-stroke/spray.

The project culminated with Tim and Brenda and their three sons climbing the ladder and gathering atop the Rock for a family photo above the words "Bren & Tim 20 years" amid a flurry of pink hearts.

We were all so proud of our accomplishment. We gathered again at the family home to recount the events of the day, congratulate one another and share pictures. Digital was still new, and Steve and I were excited to stop at the local drugstore and get eight-by-ten prints made of the family atop the rock to share with the others. I looked forward to driving by the Rock the next day to see our handiwork. After all of the times I had driven by and seen the artistry, I had never, until now, been able to look with pride at what was displayed and know that I'd had a hand, or a brush, in it.

The next morning, I got the kids off to school and headed out of town. Driving south, I had no view of the Rock because of the way the road splits along the hillside and the fir trees between the north and southbound lanes. To view it meant that I had to get off at the North Lake Samish exit, hang a left and reenter the freeway on the northbound side. Thankfully, there wasn't much traffic that morning, because I had to slow down so as not to miss it. And there it was on the Rock, as clear as day, the words "Go Jenny, Class of 2002" in bold green letters on a bright yellow background.

Growing Green—A Sustainable Courtship Between Bellingham and Me

BELLINGHAM

By Patricia L. Herlevi

In 1986, similar to prospectors of one hundred years earlier, I left Bellingham and headed to Seattle, where I hoped to strike gold in the emerging music industry. I had written my first few songs, had a decent voice and my guitar playing had improved during college. I took one last look at Bellingham as my car glided onto Interstate-5, leaving Georgia Pacific and my university years in the dust. I possessed no knowledge of Bellingham's history, of its boom and bust years and its pioneers who stripped the hills of giant cedars and diminished salmon populations in the name of commerce. Yet I too felt strained after breathing in pollutants for four years.

In the years after Bellingham and I parted, both the city and I underwent a transformation, including a "green" makeover. Bellingham and I dealt with the impact of polluting industries on our respective bodies. During the late 1990s, in Seattle, my music career came to an end when I began suffering from an environmental illness akin to a canary sent into a coal mine. At the same time, my eyes opened to the natural beauty around me. While petrochemicals and cigarette smoke wreaked havoc on my lungs and nervous and immune systems, my environmental awareness grew. An internal protest occurred inside my body, removing me from mainstream thinking and toward the hopes of a greener future, one I wouldn't find in Seattle, snarled in heavy traffic.

Eventually, after enduring two decades of Seattle's growing pains, I relocated to Mount Vernon in 2007, having heard the call of the mighty Skagit. Earlier, I had started a tradition of walking a labyrinth to end the year. After researching labyrinths in the area, I found a good one in Bellingham. I had not set foot in Bellingham for twenty-one years, and I still remembered the sulfur-tinged air and empty storefronts in the decimated downtown of the 1980s. When I stepped off the bus, I felt disoriented by an abundance of mom and pop businesses that had developed in my absence. The city's vibrant makeover with its brightly painted homes left me close to tears. Seeking a landmark in this new land, I searched the skyline for the Moorish tower of Mount Baker Theatre and the unforgettable Second Empire–style building that houses the Whatcom History and Art Museum.

The new Bellingham reminded me of the high school geek who undergoes a makeover, transforming him into an unrecognizable heartthrob. While I might have looked over Bellingham in the past, the city now drew me to it; this attraction revived my hopes of preserving a delicate balance between the city's supernatural beauty and the emergence of a green economy. However, the flirtation phase between the city and me lasted nearly four years before I decided to commit. The city and I reunited under a joint cause.

When I did return to Bellingham as a resident four years later, the only apartment I could find was two blocks from the apartment house where I lived in 1986 on North Garden Street. My memory of the day in June 1986, when I packed my few belongings, strapped my mattress to the top of my Datsun and sped my way to Seattle lingered when I moved back to this neighborhood.

As I grew another shade of green, in the summer of 2009 I visited a household in Bellingham's Birchwood neighborhood. A small group of bicyclists who joined a Sustainable Bellingham bike tour of permaculture—a closed-loop lifestyle that mimics nature—households in the city, completed their tour at the Birchwood home culminating in a potluck. The sun sent out its strong rays as the bicyclists gathered in the garden. A bear-sized dog roamed around the hens, and roosters strutted in a garden plot. At that time, I didn't know yet about Bellingham's twenty-three distinct neighborhoods and had not seen the PBS documentary *Fixing the Future Now* that featured Bellingham among other sustainable cities, so I wasn't aware I walked upon earth that had been mined of its fossil fuels. I just felt peaceful joining likeminded people.

During the winter of 2012, when I worked on a magazine assignment about permaculture homes in Bellingham, I returned to the same Birchwood home. As Christy Nieto, co-owner of the home, gave me a tour of the grounds, she mentioned old mining shafts in the neighborhood, introduced me to her free-range chickens and showed me the plots she and her partner created to grow their food. She mentioned the neighborhood's coal mining past, saying that Bellingham has long been known for its progressive attitude, and these days the progressives rally to preserve their laidback sustainable lifestyles.

Bellingham built itself from the bounty of the earth's natural resources, such as coal, wood and salmon, as well as cultivation of tulips, sugar beets and other crops with varying degrees of success. The coal mines in Birchwood extended hundreds of miles and employed 250 miners who dug 200,000 tons of coal yearly from 1917 until 1955, with the peak years in the 1920s, according to a real estate site. Bellingham Coal Mines in Birchwood weren't the only coal mines in the Bellingham area—mines in the Sehome Neighborhood, where I now live, also come to mind. I doubt Christy's hens sensed the mine shafts underneath their feet as they pecked on the ground for insects. However, I felt changes trembling beneath my muddy boots.

I learned from the Whatcom History and Art Museum archives that in addition to the Bellingham Coal Mine, Olympic Portland Cement Company and a timber mill also operated out of what composes the Birchwood Neighborhood. Other industries included a chicken hatchery and egg cooperative—urban farmers who raised chickens on one-acre plots. I wonder if unease between the small egg farmers and the big industries ever surfaced the way tension between big industry and Bellingham activists does now.

Walking through this neighborhood in 2012, past Albertsons where the mine entrance once stood, past the cheaply built apartment complexes on Northwest and West Maplewood and urban farming plots, points out contradictions still present in this otherwise vibrant neighborhood. Other Bellingham neighborhoods dealt with contradictions and controversy too, from the red-light districts of the Depression years on State Street and Railroad Avenue to the paper mill's air pollution that lingered downtown and in neighborhoods bordering the waterfront in the later years.

The cheap housing that acts as an eyesore in Birchwood and attracts transient renters points back to the housing built during the early industrial years for laborers. Certainly, seeing a shopping center pop up where an entrance to a coal mine once existed promotes commerce. However, sightings of backyard chickens and raised beds with chard and kale creeping over the edges send minds reeling back to the city's early urban farming days. Christy and her sustainable neighbors follow in a tradition that dates back one hundred years and reverberates throughout the city. This past also supported sustainable cooperatives for eggs, wool and other necessities.

Today, mirroring that, we see small intentional housing and urban farming cooperatives forming, as well as the Community Food Coop, with its two locations, which plays a significant role in community building.

Since discovering this northwest Bellingham neighborhood, I have met Birchwood residents who exude pride for their neighborhood, which these days features tree-lined streets and renovated older houses on large lots. The history of the coal mines comes up in conversations, for it's a history not easily forgotten thanks to the coal trains traveling through Whatcom County to Vancouver, British Columbia. SSA Marine and Goldman Sachs, along with Peabody Energy, propose to build a terminal at Cherry Point (Ferndale) that would ship fifty-four million tons of bulk goods (mainly coal) a year to China, a disaster to a sustainable vision for Bellingham.

While victory gardens appear in Bellingham neighborhoods that once supported coal mines, "no coal" signs mushroom on damp lawns across the city and appear in apartment windows, making me wonder how many people sporting these signs know about Bellingham's industrial past. When I first heard about the nine coal trains, each a mile long, traveling through Western Washington every day, I had no knowledge of Bellingham's own coal mining past.

Looking back to the 1980s when I attended Western Washington University, I recall choking on the rotten-egg smell of Georgia Pacific's pulp and paper mill. I had some awareness Bellingham was built on the exploitation of the land. I could see the results gazing at the scarred hillsides where trees were over-harvested, especially near Lake Samish and the view from Interstate 5.

While Bellingham now has cleaner air, provides greenways for recreationists and preserves historical neighborhoods, we catch the reminders of the past shaping our future. Strolling throughout the city, I see traces in the form of mansions of the logger and coal barons. Street signs call attention to the city's entrepreneurs and founders—Roeder, Peabody or heroes like Captain George Pickett, as in the Pickett Bridge that crosses Whatcom Creek. Strolling through the neighborhoods that hug the waterfront offers a history lesson about Bellingham's industrial experiences. Ghosts of the city's founders and exploited workers on their way to building a Pacific Northwest empire hover nearby too. They whisper in my ears. Yet I don't honor what these men built, even if the historic buildings catch my eye and cause me to pull out my digital camera or my notepad.

I was born of another consciousness focused on healing the earth rather than leaving more gashes and scars. Having spent my early childhood during

The historic York neighborhood, 2012.

the hippie era and then taking an environmental studies class while I attended Western Washington University, my battle cry invoked sustainability. Growing up during the 1960s and 1970s, I cut my teeth on *Bambi*, *The Lorax* and TV episodes of Jacques Cousteau's adventures. Before the arrival of the Internet, I perused back issues of *National Geographic*, which both celebrated the enchantment of the natural world and reported on the desecration of the planet. Closer to home, my generation and previous ones missed out on seeing the legendary giant cedar and one-hundred-pound salmon that once swam in the creeks here. I still resent this loss.

My lineages include people who came to the United States prospecting a better life and even people who dug for coal in the depths of the earth, but none of my ancestors places me in a position of atoning for the deeds of Bellingham's founders. Topping that off, I'm a person of color whom the white settlers would have shunned one hundred—even sixty—years ago. We have come a long way, it seems, but we have only traveled in a circle. What goes around comes back to slap us on the face, and now we will finally determine who wins the great debate: Mother Earth or big commerce. I know where I stand, on the other side of the picket fence with the urban deer also laying claim to this city.

———•+••+•———

When I decided to commit to Bellingham, the city teased me, hanging the "green" carrot in front of my face and luring me on wild goose chases. Decent and affordable housing remained elusive during my four-month search, yet I probably saw more of Bellingham on foot than car-driving residents who have lived here for decades. And the more I saw, the stronger my desire grew to set up home in this corner of the state.

Finally, on a rainy September day, victorious, I packed my belongings and headed north. Several truckloads later, I finally succumbed to Bellingham's charm. However, this time, I plan on staying and getting to know my community. And with the seeds we plant now, perhaps the giant cedar will return in one thousand years.

Walking Bellingham

BELLINGHAM

By Rebecca Helm Beardsall

A clairvoyant in a small coastal town in New Zealand told me walking would solve my slow—almost nonexistent—metabolism. Pounding the pavement has provided me with muscular legs and a healthy outlook on life. I walk at a fast pace, which annoys my husband, who likes to stroll. I've tried on many occasions to slow my pace for his comfort, but as soon as I stop thinking about it, my pace quickens and he is complaining we are walking too fast. I always thought my long, quick strides were freakish until Geoff and I went to visit my friend in Germany. Kerstin is at least ten inches taller than me with legs that go on for miles. However, our strides easily matched each other's; it wasn't until we were walking the streets in Bremen that I realized how natural this pace was for her. When we finally realized Geoff was no longer with us—that he was a mere speck in the distance—we decided to have a hot chocolate in a café while he caught up. When he finally arrived, I said, "I figured it out. It is my German genes that make me walk like there is no tomorrow."

So when we moved to Bellingham, Washington, from Quakertown, Pennsylvania, I was thrilled to be living in a pedestrian-friendly city boasting proper crosswalks and sidewalks. We loved the fact that we could have a nice conversation while walking from our studio apartment on Illinois Street to downtown because we didn't have to keep an eye out for cars. Prior to our move to Washington, we were staying at my parents' in Sellersville, Pennsylvania, where we no longer had the luxury of sidewalks and where we constantly had to stand aside from the road to let the cars pass. My walking life at our house in Quakertown wasn't much better; sidewalks forced me to walk the same loop. So this change of pace—being able to walk everywhere and anytime—made Bellingham a new kind of heaven.

Our daily walks shifted from happening during the bright morning sun to the dusk when Geoff started his job. We walked to Mallard Ice Cream after dinner to get a scoop of coconut sorbet. We walked to the 1300 block of Bay Street to enjoy the music at Downtown Sounds on Wednesday nights. We packed a picnic dinner to enjoy at Elizabeth Park on Thursdays for the Park Concert Series. On weekends, we walked to Mount Bakery for breakfast before heading to the farmers market where the bountiful harvest and the creativity of the Pacific Northwest surrounded us. After gathering fresh produce, which always included our newfound delight—sunflower sprouts—we took a leisurely walk home exploring different neighborhoods. This exploration was part of our daily house hunting.

In addition to our walks, I daily scoured the Internet and sent endless e-mails to our realtor about houses. We looked at many houses downtown in the Colombia and Cornwall neighborhoods. The Colombia neighborhood, part of the Fountain District and one of Bellingham's oldest neighborhoods, boasts quaint Craftsman-style homes. Cornwall is the neighborhood adjacent to Columbia. Both neighborhoods have turn-of-the-century homes, are close to parks and shops and are within easy walking distance to town. Several things held us back from making an offer; either the house was in our price range but in desperate need of repair and remodeling, or it was beautifully remodeled and well out of our price range. Geoff started talking about looking outside of downtown for houses. I became depressed about the situation—seeing my dreams of living within walking distances slip away. I refused to consider this option. Geoff, however, was relentless and started talking about a trail system near the Barkley neighborhood. I continued to ignore him and tried to find a house in Columbia.

Finally, Geoff said we needed to go for a drive in the Barkley area one weekend; instead of venturing to the farmers market, we got in the car—the car!—to check out the Barkley area of Bellingham. Sitting in the warm car, my resolve dug in even more—I did not want to live somewhere where I could not walk to everything. I was grumpy and refused to see anything good about the area. Geoff pointed out that there was a shopping center, Barkley Village, with a grocery store within walking distance, to which I replied, "Yes, but the houses are all uphill." I drove the car up the hill and kept saying, "This is too far away." For every complaint I had, Geoff answered with something about trails, and he told me to pull over so he could ask about the

This marker is located at the entrance to Railroad Trail.

trails. I said, "We can't ask a kid. He shouldn't be talking to strangers." Again my complaints were ignored. Geoff asked the young boy on his scooter if there was a trail nearby. "Yeah." The kid answered pointing down the hill. "How long does it take to walk the trail to the grocery store?" "I dunno. Maybe five minutes." "Thanks!" We drove away. Finally Geoff couldn't take it anymore and said we had to go on the trails. I parked the car, but not my bad attitude. "I'm in flip-flops. I can't go walking trails." "Come on…"

On this steep hill, we followed a little twisting trail down. Then we walked into the main trail, and it was like hearing angels sing. My jaw dropped, and I scanned the trail and said, "This is amazing…Yes, let's move to Barkley." It was that simple. The trails sold me. A canopy of trees covered the pathway, and the banks were filled with foliage from ferns to blackberry bushes. The walk to the grocery store was short, just like the boy said. We saw so many people on the trail—people riding bikes, walking dogs, running or strolling. As we walked back up the hill, I was planning my new life on the trails. I noticed trail makers stating Whatcom Falls, Big Rock Park and other fabulous Bellingham parks.

We got back in the car, and now I was the one telling Geoff to stop the car as I spotted another house for sale. When we crossed Barkley Boulevard, we saw our house. We both decided, just by looking on the outside and reading the blurb on the flyer, that this was the one. "Unless there is something majorly wrong with it inside, this is our house," I said to Geoff as we walked around to check out the back. When we were looking at the place, the neighbor came out on his deck and asked if we were looking at the house. Then he said, "Do you like to walk?"

"Yes!"

"There are great trails around here."

—◆◆◆◆◆—

On the day that we put an offer in on the house, we decided to take a walk to Whatcom Falls from our soon-to-be new house. We took the small, winding trail across the street that linked with the Railroad Trail. This time, instead of heading west toward Barkley Village, we turned east, heading toward Lake Whatcom. The eastern trail is more wooded and feels like walking in the wilderness, as if any second a mountain lion might appear. The trees and shrubs create the perfect illusion of seclusion. On a hot, sunny day, walking under the trees was refreshing. We soon came to the Alabama pedestrian bridge that sits high above the road in the middle of Alabama Hill. From the bridge, there is an amazing panoramic view of downtown Bellingham and the bay. We stood there admiring our new city, pointing out the old city hall, now a museum, and Mount Baker Theatre. We continued on our walk. The closer we got to the falls, the more people we saw. I started noticing kids riding their bikes in soaking wet clothing. I assumed they were swimming at Bloedel Donovan Park, the public swimming hole. However, as we started winding our way toward the falls on the dark, dirt trails, we noticed people wading out into the cold water. We were shocked to see entire families wading into the water and jumping off the falls.

—◆◆◆◆◆—

Soon after our move into the house, Bellingham was hosting the Bite of Bellingham—a downtown food festival. We were planning on meeting friends there and were walking down to catch the bus. However, when we reached

View of the city from the Alabama walking bridge.

the bus stop, we realized we had just missed the bus and had to wait another thirty minutes; since it was the weekend, the buses weren't on their normal fifteen-minute schedule. As we stood there discussing our options, once again Geoff mentioned the trails. We had never taken the trails downtown, and I was apprehensive about whether we would make it in time to meet our friends, but with the thirty-minute wait for the bus, we decided the trails were our best option.

This time, it wasn't the towering trees surrounding us, but instead there were blackberry bushes on every side of the trail. "Look at all those glorious blackberries," Geoff said, grabbing one from the bush and eating it. "Don't do that!" my worrying ways shouted in my head. First, I thought, what if they aren't blackberries and instead are some rare poisonous berry from the West Coast? Second, who do the bushes belong to? As we walked around the corner of the trail, we saw a young woman with a blue Tupperware dish already full of berries and another bowl in her hand. "It is blackberry season," she sang in a melodious voice. We smiled and kept walking. As soon as we were out of earshot, I whispered to Geoff, "You can just pick the berries!" They didn't belong to anyone. They belonged to everyone.

As we approached one section of the trail, we heard traffic noise and wondered where we were. Emerging from the blackberry bushes, we arrived at I-5. We walked across the pedestrian bridge, stopping to take a few photos. We felt so secluded on the trails, even so close to the bustle of the highway. However, the whole walk toward town we were talking about blackberries—free blackberries! We made it a point to venture out the next day with a bowl.

I shared this knowledge with my friend Dusti. So this year we both set out from our respective houses at 1:00 p.m. walking the Railroad Trail, knowing that if our timing was just right we would meet in the middle of the perfect place to pick blackberries. Sure enough, as I rounded the corner, there were Dusti and her three girls, who already had purple, berry-stained fingers. As we picked berries, we listened to the girls' chatter and allowed the summer sun to soak into our skin. I thought I was sharing some insider information with Dusti since they had just recently moved to this part of Bellingham and their new house was right on Railroad Trail. She informed me of other places along the trails to pick apples and plums. Plums so ripe and sweet they melted in our mouths. Plums Geoff and I would stuff in his backpack on a bike ride home after having breakfast downtown.

———◆◆◆◆◆———

Walking the trails to Fairhaven with a view of the bay and San Juan Islands.

As my love of the trail system has grown, so has my love of Bellingham and the community here. The trails mirror the larger community as we follow rules of protocol—a bike bell means move to the right, a smile or nod to a runner is sufficient, a "hello" is more appropriate to strolling friends. On one of my first commutes home on the trail system, I stopped at a crosswalk to change the song on my iPod when I saw a dog come running out of the trail followed by his owner running behind him and then heard a "Hi, Rebecca." I looked up to see my friend from Fountain Parish as she continued on her way. This was the first time I actually met someone I knew on the trails. Sadly, my delayed reaction meant I was unable to reciprocate the greeting. My community is no longer just where I work and live—it is also where I walk. One day on Railroad Trail, I noticed a cute little black and white dog and thought, I know that dog…it looks like Sandy. And sure enough, following Sandy was her family riding their bikes. I called out, "Hello, Holley!" This time I was the one shouting out a hello, and the sense of home settled into my heart.

A Tag Team of Memories—Remember that Time in Seattle?

SEATTLE

By Marjorie Maddox and Gary R. Hafer

I. Margie

Unlike most things in our marriage, Seattle was spontaneous. Choosing it, getting there, aligning ourselves with both its leisure and adventure—the city itself full of who we are together and apart.

At the time, my sister worked for a large hotel chain. With the surprise of a ten-year-old performing a magic trick that actually works, she could produce a $400 luxury room in this city or that. The cost? The freedom to say *yes* and a mere $35 a night. Still, we had to plan the freedom. As new college professors, our lives were brimming over with books, assignments, freshmen essays and committee meetings. Shackled with both university and self-imposed deadlines, we considered any getaway impossible. Although we complained often about the few cultural choices in our small Pennsylvania town, we rarely had the time or energy to venture outside the tiny offices in our also tiny rented duplex. "So much to do, so much to do," we mused, but none of it restful or exciting.

Yes, we had to plan the freedom—but not too much. Mostly, we had to rearrange our minds to make room for choices. We had spring and summer breaks and—although at this point in our almost twenty-year marriage, it's hard to remember—no children. Why couldn't we pick up and go someplace that spoke to our hearts? Why couldn't we—suddenly, spontaneously—decide at the end of summer to travel to Seattle, a city, the travel brochures promised, of calm rains, calm bookstores and calm coffeehouses where we could leisurely sip our favorite roast and reconnect with what we most wanted to be. Of all the piles of color travel guides that I kept stacked beside our bed, the one on Seattle most offered that calm. It also offered adventure: a trek halfway across the country to a city we'd never seen, the allure of the waterfront, the mystery and history of the Underground, the quick pulse of a "real" night life.

But first we had to get there.

II. Gary

And getting to any major city was always a struggle. Flying from a small Pennsylvania town to anywhere meant laying out printed maps and schedules for connecting flights on the dining room table, considering cities we wouldn't dread spending a few hours in if we missed the connections and had to wait in their airports. I had no skills for the matrix such scheduling required. But that's what Margie knew best. She says often in conversations with friends that she can't "do math," but here she was, quoting flight take offs and arrivals like an Englishman with train schedules. She excelled at all the practical math problems involved.

Not that she left me out of the equation. She barraged our newly married life with questions on what I preferred—a connection in Pittsburgh or Philadelphia, this scenic tour or this harbor cruise, lavishly detailed in a ten-page brochure. I wasn't the traveler or the mathematician—or the decider—but I was an excellent delegator. I let Margie route us to Pittsburgh, rather than Philadelphia, because every reason she gave seemed right to me, the uninitiated. "Whatever."

So a week later, we arrived bleary-eyed in Seattle, having taken a red-eye flight west from Pittsburgh. The skies that greeted us were blue and the sun too bright. I thought it always rained in Seattle as we picked up our luggage filled with umbrellas and rain gear.

After a shuttle to the hotel and a quick unpack, we walked down to the hotel breakfast bar, where we sat and stared into each other's eyes—blood-red eyes, that is. I wondered if the Mariners were in town.

III. Margie

Were they? I don't remember the Mariners or if we went to see them. Nor do I remember the breakfast bar or the blood-red eyes. Or rather, now sharing these same descriptions in so many cities and travels, I can't remember which were specific to Seattle and which just a part of our overall travel rituals. What I do remember, though, is the sense of possibility: a town with coffee, crabs and cruises.

Of course, being in Seattle, we had to start with coffee. After downing our cups of joe at the breakfast bar, we headed out for more of Seattle's finest. What better place to get both our freshly ground java and our freshly caught seafood than Pike's Fish Market? Surely, with just a tad bit of help from a city map, we could follow our noses. The aroma would be everywhere. We only needed to point ourselves in the right direction and go.

Not so fast—or so easy. If we had been wise enough to let our tired feet decide before rushing to this decision, surely all four of them would have contested. Even at our first meeting, we got lost. This turned out to be a good thing since—on "break" at an English convention in Pennsylvania—the process of driving in circles to get from Point A to Point B gave us time to talk and talk some more. If either one of us would have known or cared where exactly we were going, would we have ended up where we are now? I don't think so.

And so six or so years after that first meeting, now married and trudging up and down Seattle's neighborhood streets, we were, once again, trying to find our way. There was no matching the small space we studied on the map and what felt like the very large spaces our legs were stretching. There was no connecting the map's confident "You Are Here!" printed near the hotel we had abandoned and the "You Have Arrived!" that we envisioned hanging above a café table boasting steaming coffee and crab cakes. But on we walked.

What we stumbled upon en route was joy. I don't remember which side street it was on or how we found it, but in the midst of nowhere, it seemed, came the oasis of a bookstore. Elsewhere, the stores and their titles would live on every street corner, luring us in with their seductive spines. But we weren't elsewhere. We were, well, someplace in Seattle, trying to head to someplace else in Seattle. And here was a respite. Here was who we were in the middle of not knowing where—exactly—we were. We entered with glee.

And stayed for hours. There is an otherworldliness that pervades any bookstore, but especially one in a new city, and perhaps even more especially in Seattle, the king of all booksellers. Rows and rows greeted me with poetry, stories and more travel possibilities. From a metal case near the front, I could journey to Ireland, Egypt or Nigeria. Halfway back on an overstuffed couch flanked by pine shelves, I could read my way into the life of Queen Victoria, Virginia Woolf or Gandhi. Even the posters scattered above faded armchairs promised cozy exchanges with authors at upcoming book signings. With my cup of free coffee in hand, I had only to turn a page to be off to new places and ideas. This, I often think, is me at my happiest: in the very good company of very good books. What could be better?

I was soon reminded. Looking across the shop, I saw Gary enveloped in the same otherworldliness. On a contented mission to discover a new reading adventure, he had forgotten his tired feet. He had forgotten the already well-worn map. He probably also had already forgotten me as I momentarily had forgotten him.

And yet, this was exactly what united us. In some ways, we are very different individuals. I prefer the outdoors; he prefers the indoors. I tend toward optimism (unrealistic idealism he might say); he toward pessimism (downright negativism, I might counter). Yet, despite our different tendencies, we were there in that bookstore in that literary city for a reason. Our great love of reading pulled us closer and kept us together, this time punctuated by the purring of the espresso machine in one out-of-the-way Seattle bookstore.

And so, fortified by espresso, new books and fresh conversations, we journeyed on to seafood. The second leg of the journey seemed shorter, and soon we were indeed following our noses—and our ears and eyes. The aroma of pike, cod, salmon and crab was strong, but the strumming of street musicians was just as strong, in tune somehow with the peddlers hawking white fish and chips. The neon sign—Public Market—obvious even when unlit in daylight hours—dared anyone to ignore what couldn't be ignored: the very hustle and bustle of Seattle.

Here were the "fish guys" spontaneously hurling two-foot sockeye back-and-forth over counters. (Or was the spontaneity merely planned for the tourists' cameras? The same way we planned the spontaneity of Seattle?) What existed in those moments among the jovial fish guys was akin to the miraculous. Between each heave and toss, I held my breath. Waiting. Expecting. Would we be greeted with a loud thud? With fish guts and eyes sprawled across the market floor? Never!

Nearby, bakers tempted our tongues with stacks of sticky buns. Teenagers with dirty aprons displayed their bowls of oysters. Old women held up for our inspection their carefully crocheted dog sweaters. Through everything was woven the accent of immigrant and native, young and old.

Half a block down, pyramids of fresh fruit balanced like acrobats, and real acrobats, dressed up like fresh fruit, somersaulted through the air. It was all part of the show, 19½ hours a day, 362 days a year. We knew it had started in 1907 with just a handful of farmers, but nothing prepared us for the vast expanse of food and craft—nine acres of stands spread so much farther than our morning's bookstore rows.

We gasped and *ahh*-ed with all the other tourists. We nodded knowingly with the locals. And then we remembered we were hungry and sat down for that additional cup of coffee and crab cake supplemented by "Famous Pike Market Chowder." We had, after all, been thinking about it a good part of the morning.

IV. Gary

The craft brew industry started on the West Coast, and the new wave—at least in the Pacific Northwest—was the rediscovery of the darker beers. (Perhaps Margie thinks my pessimism took on corporeal form.) I was eager to taste the dark old ales that I had read about in trade magazines, so it wasn't long into our meandering walking tour of the city that I spotted a saloon with an antique neon sign. We wandered in and took seats right at the bar, large brass vats now standing at attention in front of us. What seems commonplace in any midscale city was, nevertheless, the innovation then.

I remember the smooth espresso stout that I sipped for the first time. Its foam was ample, like the generic Guinness, but tan instead of white. The strong coffee taste dominated. My face, then dark-bearded, rehearsed a foam mustache, Margie joining me with her half pint. In the sparse lighting, made darker by the wooden paneling, we inspected ourselves in the large wall mirror behind the bar, foam mustaches above our mutual grins.

V. Margie

We emerged from the dimly lit brewery into the (once again) surprising brightness of Seattle. While we were inside nursing our espresso stouts, the skies had acquiesced to a crisp cleansing rain. Now, though, only puddles remained beneath a bold mid-afternoon sun. We breathed in the famously clean air and resumed our earlier walk, enjoying the warmth while we could. Within an hour's time, we would descend into a dank, dark world of a bygone Seattle. Yes, we were headed to the Underground.

I wasn't sure if Gary was humoring me or was genuinely interested, but ever since I had first heard of the strange catacomb-like passageways, I was intrigued. The Underground boasted the shady yarns of late-night movies and Poe-like mystery. Not coincidentally, it was another poet at a writing conference who first spun for me the city's history. At the time, it seemed pure fiction. I imagined serial killers chasing screaming women through shadowy labyrinths. I envisioned scheming con men and conniving madams.

Here was a city beneath a city, a city that—for years—town members had dismissed as mere rumor. Here was a town foolish in its inception built as it was on filled-in flood plains, where, almost comically, toilets flushed backward. Here was a community hammered together with tall tales, tragedy and triumph: the Great Seattle Fire, not unlike our own Centralia, Pennsylvania mine fires, snaking beyond control; the Yukon Gold Rush, with its 100,000 adventurers clamoring for booze and euphemistically named "seamstresses"; a community shunned and condemned, the fear of bubonic plague hovering everywhere.

And so it was into these various "stories" we descended several "stories"—twelve feet or more—leaving behind Pioneer Square, Elliott Bay and the entire twentieth century, except, of course, for the tour guides. Both historical and contemporary in their entrepreneurship, they expertly led us not only through the secret passageways of the town's past but also through a tour of human depression and depravity: flophouses, speakeasies, opium dens. It all seemed an elaborate metaphor: sink to your lowest common denominator, cover it up, deny it ever existed.

Yet even within that dismal injunction was the architecture of hope: anything can be rebuilt. Even a city. Even a life. Now, almost twenty years into our marriage, I think back on the pure bravado of Seattle's scheme. Start again. Keep what you have. Build on top.

Before I had met Gary, I had done just that: picked up, moved halfway across the country and started again. I love that Gary and I now can do this together. While we have only the desire to travel, not move, across country, we do continue building our lives—sometimes in surprising ways. No, we don't have the overall unstable foundation of a Seattle, but we have plummeted into the sinkholes of health scares. We have, like everyone else, toppled from our own shortsightedness. But we also have kept the bricks and mortar coming, building up, out, around, always restructuring—to the best of our abilities—this odd-shaped cityscape called marriage.

VI. Gary

Of course, our city of a marriage wasn't made in a day. Early in our marriage, I exemplified the stereotypical husband in not remembering much.

I know Margie remembers in a vivid picture to my thumbnail sketch. I could attribute such forgetfulness to my old age, but I assign it to that early period in our marriage when we did not have two children and time seemed endless. During that time, I let memories slide into forgetfulness because there would be so many more to come, all so similar as to defy distinction. Or so I thought. But that's the arrogance of youth—perhaps my youth alone—that didn't ponder the driving in circles or seeing the acrobats perform in open air, which I just faintly recall. Today, I can vividly remember—and treasure—a one-day getaway with my wife, just one town over from home, not because it is recent, but because I know there will be fewer memories to make with my wife. I feel each time with her is now unique; I am saddened when the time passes all too quickly, but mostly that I've just come to this conclusion in the past year. Our children, as wonderful as they are, ration those special times with my wife—infrequent though they are—as they are crowded out with children's recitals, baseball games and doctor appointments.

Looking back now, it's hard for me to believe that the sunset cruise we took seemed like an everyday event. True, such cruises are standard tourist fare of any portside city, regardless of which coast. Yet there we were, tourists on a ninety-minute ship ride, the top level serving as a flat observation deck to see the city and the beautiful skyline. A large full moon had just risen over the ocean, the waves calmly dancing with the light the moon cast on it. We talked little. Margie clung tightly to me as a second sweater against the cool ocean breeze that seemed to change directions the farther we pulled away from land. We walked on the top deck, the moon casting our long shadows onto each other against the dim moonlight.

The cruise ended in precisely the ninety minutes without crew narration and noisy tourist chatter. We disembarked and walked down a long loading platform onto the street. We had planned to walk back to the hotel, but looking out that cool summer evening, the night greeted us as silently as the ocean had. The sounds I knew of cities—the sirens from screaming ambulances and reverberations from low-flying aircraft—were eerily absent. I heard only the slow, steady hum of taxis parked next to us, arranged in single file like schoolchildren waiting for something to happen. I counted twenty taxis snaking through the winding street, waiting. But why?

Then my eyes confirmed what I should have known from my ears. I saw no one walking, no cars driving by.

We stepped into the street and felt a rush of folks from the cruise all run past us, all fanning in different directions but seeming purposeful in knowing where they wanted to go. Except us.

"I'm not so sure this is a good idea," I said hesitantly, influenced, perhaps, by more than one of the horror stories from the Underground tour.

"*What* is not a good idea?" Margie wanted to know.

I wasn't sure of my language or my thinking, so I rehearsed them again with Margie. "I think we should take a cab."

Margie seemed puzzled. "I thought you said we could walk to the hotel from here. Is it too far after all? I'm not sure where the hotel is. I'm all turned around."

She hadn't perceived our surroundings after dark the same way I had. "It isn't that we *can't* walk it," I replied. "I just think we *shouldn't* walk it."

I gestured with both hands, right and left spanning. "There's no one on the streets."

She nodded. Just as I had done when we first planned our trip, it was now Margie's turn to say, "Whatever." She led the way as we grabbed about the tenth taxi in line.

Margie told the driver the hotel address, and we were off. We passed through a series of green traffic lights, up a long street that climbed skyward. There were no red lights. Neither were there any people on the streets, even though it was just around 8:00 p.m. Where was the hopping night life from the travel brochures? From the backseat of the cab, every intersection invited us to move along with its green lights. We each manned a side passenger window to stare at the long, wide streets, marked with pedestrian lines and signs, all uninhabited. I saw just one person on that ride through the city: a lone homeless man curled around a newspaper vending machine, slouched and sleeping.

The driver, voiceless until arriving at the hotel, now announced loudly, "This is your hotel."

Margie and I slid across the seats and exited to the right. I stuck my head in the open window of the front passenger side to give the driver a twenty-dollar bill; when he returned the change, I returned half. He left us without a word, Margie and I now standing on the step of the hotel, its awning lights bright. The doorman had already opened a passage for us. Margie stepped inside, but I stopped. For one moment, I turned to review the streets we had just escaped to see no one at all.

Above: From the observation deck of Seattle's Space Needle.

Left: Outside our Seattle hotel, soon to return to our "other" lives.

VII. Margie

I had wanted it to last. I had wanted to debark from that cruise ship and leisurely, romantically, stroll on that calm summer night back to the hotel. Maybe we would stop somewhere en route for that famous Seattle night life and dance our tired feet off in a loud club with music blaring. Maybe we would pause for a nightcap or a quiet cup of decaf in a trendy café. The next day, we would take in the view of the entire city from atop the Seattle Space Needle and then ferry across to Victoria for high tea. Too soon, we would be soaring back to our other life. Too soon.

But then the deserted streets stared us down. And won. The emptiness sent us quickly on our way.

On West Kinnear—The Life and Death of a Seattle House

SEATTLE

By Lauren D. McKinney

M r. and Mrs. Frederick V. Betts, 700 West Kinnear Place, Seattle NW, Wash." is how I addressed the thank-you notes as a small child. Each time I scratched the address on the Crane's envelope with my cartridge pen, I pictured my great-aunt and great-uncle reading the note, sitting on the porch or in the parlor, view of the Sound and the downtown in the picture windows. From what I had heard, the house, from which so many Christmas and birthday gifts originated, overlooked the city.

Fred was my grandmother Genevieve's youngest brother, and they had grown up in the house beginning in 1906, when my grandmother was seven. That's when her father, a banker, had been transferred from Syracuse. My grandmother, whom I called Nana, would show me sepia-colored photographs of 700 West Kinnear and tell me stories of her childhood there. She remembers when Fred was born in the northwest bedroom. Aunt Laura lived in the room next to that, and in another room lived an ailing grandmother, who banged the floor with her cane when she wanted something. Nana had her own room, and the three brothers shared one. The big house was full.

It's a turreted Victorian with a commanding wraparound porch, and when my mother was a child, she pretended the porch was the deck of a ship. She was almost as familiar with the house as Nana was because when Nana divorced, she and my mother lived there in the 1930s. It had a great capacity to take people in. I have several pictures of unidentified people standing in the yard or on the porch and plenty of my mother with her tousled Little Rascals look and her doll baby carriage. In another picture, little Fred glowers from a real baby carriage. In another, Nana, a laughing sixteen-year-old in a sailor dress, plays with their collie Ky. The photos, loose in a box, jumbled the decades together, but the house was always in the background, its presence linking all the animals and children and grownups together.

My first visit was the summer I graduated from high school, 1976, with my mother and grandmother, and I returned on my own in 1986, again with a close friend in 1990 and with my new husband in 1998. Aunt Arline fussed over us in 1976, but by 1985, she was gone. Until a year before his death in 2002, Fred lived alone, puttering in the rose garden, pruning the apple trees and repairing the creaking but ever solid house, the house

Above: Lauren's great-grandmother Grace Betts with her collie Ky, circa 1916.

Opposite: Lauren's great-uncle Fred; her mother, Nancy; and her great-grandmother Grace in the mid-1940s.

he had been born in, the only house he had ever called his own.

The house at 700 West Kinnear was a masculine yellow, bordering on tan, windows sternly trimmed in brown. This color scheme never varied. Situated on a sharply triangular lot, the house was flanked by an apple orchard on the shortest side of the triangle, close to the neighbors. The hypotenuse is West Kinnear Place, and the third side is West Prospect Street. A wall rises on the other side of West Prospect, and above that wall is Willard Avenue. When my grandmother was a teenager, she used to sneak out of the house on the

Sabbath to play tennis on a court on Willard Avenue. Farther up the hill, wild blackberries grew in the open field. After a day at Queen Anne Grammar School, my Nana and her brothers filled their pockets with the tart berries, laughing and chasing one another in the warm September afternoon.

West Queen Anne Hill is steep, with sets of concrete steps linking the streets. One set goes up the hill from West Prospect toward Prospect Park. Another set goes down toward Olympic Place. Nana said the children used to sled down these in a rare heavy snowfall. The sharp angles of the yard and "the point," along with the stairs ascending and descending to other streets, always seemed to countermand the settled squareness of the house, as if to remind the house that everything is contingent.

Over the years, the house on West Kinnear became known for its views, and photos of the view from the porch, as seen between the columns, appeared in a glossy picture book of Seattle. And one day in Philadelphia, as I watched the 1993 movie *The Little Buddha* by myself at a matinee, I was stunned to see a long shot of the West Prospect side of the house. I knew the movie was filmed mostly in a modern house higher up on Queen Anne, but seeing Fred's house, Nana's house, "our" house as a visual prop in a movie unnerved me. My heart pounded, and for several minutes, it was hard to pay attention to the movie. A shard of my story had broken into its story.

What, I asked myself, did this place mean to me, exactly? And why was it so unsettling to see the house show up for a few seconds in *The Little Buddha*? I think that's the first time I realized that

Lauren's great-grandparents Graham and Grace Betts, circa 1916.

other people desired it, that it signified something to them, that they had noticed it. I felt jealousy.

To me, 700 West Kinnear held the past together and served as proof of my family's rootedness despite two later generations of military life. Nana's second husband and my father were both army officers. It amazed me, after all the places I had lived—Germany; Georgia; Oklahoma; Schenectady, New York—that the house still ran on the knob and tube electricity rigged up by Fred and his brothers in the 1920s. Fred didn't drink much or clean out his liquor cabinet often; I found a bottle of some kind of hard liquor that dated from 1918. Quilts my great-grandmother made, old radios that had names of Pacific Northwest radio stations on the dial, books owned by three generations shelved companionably together in barrister bookcases; whenever I visited, I inhabited the place, breathed its memories and made it mine. It didn't occur to me that someone else could make it theirs.

In the year 2000, when Fred came East for Nana's 101st birthday party, he told me that the house had been filmed again, this time for a show called *Six Feet Under*. I didn't think that much about it, but I made a mental note to see it some time. Finally, three years ago, seven years after Fred's death, as I was making my way through the series and had almost forgotten, there it was: 700 West Kinnear Place. In the episode, called "Driving Mr. Mossback," Nate and his sister Claire stay with an old friend of Nick's named Lisa. Nate and Claire pull up to the house, driving east on West Kinnear, and stop at the bottom of the concrete steps going up to the porch. "Sweet," murmurs Claire, as they walk up the steps, and she glances behind her at the view of the downtown and Mount Rainier. The view is needlessly pumped up with a telephoto lens. The porch has a letterbox on the wall. Fred's mail actually came to the back, to the kitchen door. The interior was not really Fred's house, probably filmed at the studio, but my hungry eyes couldn't help but look for clues. There were none.

Unlike the house's brief appearance in *The Little Buddha*, this was no passing shot of a house in order to establish a sense of place. It was the place itself. It was where Nate had lived in happier times. Lisa is an old flame who remains deeply in love with him, and she still keeps his shirt in the closet. I like to think that the producers of *Six Feet Under* saw something special in 700 West Kinnear: its capacious hospitality, its unrenovated simplicity or the last of Queen Anne Hill's shabby gentility. Or maybe it was just a big old house with a view, passing for bohemian with the right props. I like to think they were close to seeing its soul.

———————

In 1998, my husband and I made a special dinner for Fred. It was more gourmet than his usual steak with a pat of butter on top. We had fresh pasta with gorgonzola and a crisp salad. We bought everything, including the wine, at Pike Place Market. At some point during this dinner, we offered to renovate the third floor and live there. We would help Fred maintain the place—he was ninety-three by then and still fixing the roof himself—and my husband would get a tech job easily in Seattle. I told Fred how much we loved the house and what it meant to me.

He wrote me a sweet letter later, saying he thought it would be too hard to live with other people in the house at his age. He had a point, and I had to ask myself how serious we really were about the offer. He lived in the house until 2001, when he sold it to a dotcom millionaire and moved to a retirement community downtown. The last time I saw Uncle Fred was that year, when he flew East to attend my grandmother's 102nd birthday party. At the party, he said to me, "I should have agreed to get that house historically certified. Because I sure do hate what this guy is doing to it." According to Fred, the new owner was planning to actually move the house over a few feet, away from the orchard and toward the point, to create a new lot for another house. And he was going to renovate the house almost beyond recognition.

My grandmother died in the spring of 2002, and then Uncle Fred died on July 4 of that year. My brother Dan and I flew out for his memorial service at Plymouth Congregational Church, the church he had attended his whole life. The reminiscences of his friends and colleagues confirmed my sense of Fred. He was an all-American, self-effacing, pragmatic man, dispensing painfully firm handshakes and bear hugs into his nineties. He was a trial lawyer and a gentleman, a man of his word, a dying breed.

I stayed a few days longer to get a sense of Seattle as a place that had meant home to me. I walked all the way up to Queen Anne Hill to see the house. If the Betts family, early in the twentieth century, could walk all the way to and from church downtown, then I could walk it one way. His cousin had warned me, "You won't like what you see."

My stomach turned as I saw that the windows were boarded up. A huge semi was parked in Fred's rose garden, which had been unkempt for a year. This was not a house. It was a corpse. I walked under the old apple trees and saw that wild blackberry canes had staked their claim, with berries just beginning to ripen. A clawing grief took hold of me.

I found some tissues in my purse and rang the doorbell of a neighbor named Alexandra, who gave me old pictures of the house that she had saved. She corroborated the story about the new owner moving the house several feet so he could subdivide the part of the yard with the apple trees. She gave me tea, and we commiserated together and celebrated Fred's life.

In 2009, the house went up for sale again, this time as a house made so luxurious that no one can afford it, a house made so huge that no one can fill it. The owner after Fred had successfully moved the house and renovated down to the studs. He finished all the raw spaces. He added a gluttonous new porch and a kitchen no one will cook in. And then the owner moved on, perhaps going broke in the 2008 economic freefall. The attic, with its dusty books and old family things, is now a vast beige space covered in beige carpet. The once-utilitarian basement, with all Fred's ancient tools, is also covered in this viral beige carpet and "finished." I don't recognize the house anymore. Its soul has been surgically removed. Gone are the austerity and restraint that made the view so full of grace.

———◆•••◆———

No one living here will tinker with tools in the basement, fix his own roof or mow his own lawn. No film companies will impute bohemianism to this new place. But one thing makes me take heart. Nobody can stop the blackberries from growing like weeds in Seattle.

Siren Song

SEATTLE

By Colleen Lutz Clemens

Washington has stolen four people I love. Matt, Laura and Rebecca all moved there for love: love of a woman, love of a family and love of, well, Washington. I joke that at least one plane ticket gets me to the people I miss, but I don't find the joke funny. I want my people near me. Washington's siren song only seems to get louder as I get older.

But the first person Washington stole was also the first person I really loved. I had a lot of crushes in elementary school. I named my first dog after a boy with a sweet smile and olive skin in my kindergarten class. I wrote notes to boys in third grade. But in ninth grade, I fell in love with Marty, the tallest boy in the school, the boy who stole the ninth grade presidential election out from under the feet of the pretty girl who dared use the word "clout" on her campaign posters. He was just badass enough to frighten and entice the girls. Not exactly good-looking in the Corey Haim/River Phoenix kind of way, he wore enough Drakar Noir to elicit mockery from everyone's favorite biology teacher. Marty dressed like he could break a girl's heart with ease: leather jacket, acidy jeans, white T-shirts. But he didn't break hearts on purpose. He broke mine because he had to move back to Seattle. Pennsylvania wasn't where he belonged.

———•+•+•———

Though we were in ninth grade, Marty could already drive. He drove a brown boat of a car, no seatbelts in the back, only lap belts in the front.

Our small band of friends first experienced the freedom of the open road in that boat. Not only was Marty older than the group, but I was also younger, having started school early, the last one of my peers to be able to drive in high school or drink in college. Marty drove us to movies, to dances, to Dorney Park, to anywhere we wanted to go. I loved him in part because he had a lot to teach me and could show me the world.

But the liberation of the open road isn't what attracted me to him—it was his ability to show me how to liberate my mind that made me love him. I fancied myself a young artist and poet in middle school. I read books about Andy Warhol, had dog-eared copies of Whitman on my nightstand, sat in my room and listened to REM's *Green* album on cassette, jumping up to change the side over and over. I felt like no one understood this part of me or that no one really tried to. Marty was the first to see and admire this nascent facet of my personality.

Marty wrote. Marty read. On an early date, Marty and I saw *Dead Poet's Society*. During the opening scene, birds fly from an open field. The scene looks young, fresh, vibrant and full of promise, just as the boys in the class. Marty leaned over: "I love the cinematography in this film. It should win an award." Decades later, I recognize the importance of the scene: as an English professor, I was bred on observation and analysis, but as a thirteen-year-old, I just thought the scene was pretty. Marty never made me feel dumb or little, so I didn't feel afraid to ask him what that word meant. As he explained it to me, I saw that movies weren't just plots, that someone else—an entire person who could win an award—helped to tell the story with pictures. Though a small moment in our relationship, I see now how telling it was: Marty is now a filmmaker, and I often teach and write about film. He gave me the permission in an otherwise blue-collar world to think that art mattered. He recognized me as a fellow artist, a recognition that allowed me to even consider my passions viable, worthy.

The day Marty left to live with his father in Seattle, we sat at the front curb of my house, his long brown car parked near us. I don't remember saying goodbye. I do remember sitting out there for a long time, that my dad came out and shook Marty's hand. I remember heartbreak.

———•◦•◦•———

Marty and I talked on the phone. He suggested I come to visit him, to get on a plane by myself and fly across the country, when I had only flown to Florida with my parents as a little girl. I see my fourteen-year-old self walking down the stairwell of our town house and asking—maybe even telling—my parents I was going to see Marty. If they balked, I don't remember the moment. I made buckets of money that summer—for a fourteen-year-old, working at Dorney Park was a rite of passage and a boon to the pocketbook. But I still needed help with the plane ticket. Mom and Dad said they would help me, that I would have to draw a number out of a hat with a percentage of what they would pay, up to 50 percent. The TV was on in the living room as I looked at the hat in front of me. I reached in and pulled out a folded piece of paper: "50 percent!" I yipped. Then my mom showed me all of the papers. Each sheet read, "50 percent." Later that summer, I got on a plane and flew across the country

Seattle made me feel hip. Though the grunge scene of which I'd buy into wholeheartedly during college was already in its early stages while I was there, I saw no evidence of it. Instead, Marty's dad and girlfriend made sure I hit the highlights. They let me stay in Marty's room like I was an adult. They talked about books and art with me. They took me to a New Age store where I picked out a crystal—or let it pick me out, swinging the quartz points like talisman over my palms to see which crystal shared "my energy."

At Pike's Market, I watched the tourists, the fishmongers, the locals. I had never noticed locals before. I just was one. To see the divide between the two gave me my first glimpse of how I wanted to act when on other people's turf. I tried to act cool, to not take pictures or gawk, even though that is all I wanted to do. Though I didn't have much money, I admired a pair of silver drop earrings dangling a blue stone. I bought the earrings as my souvenir. Twenty years later, those earrings still come out of the jewelry box sometimes.

We drove to the top of Mount Rainier. I didn't realize then that a beautiful day with a full view from the top is rare. When I see cars boasting "I went up Mount Rainier" bumper stickers, I remember the day we climbed up and up in a car without seat belts, me pressed against Marty in the back seat. I had never been on a mountain that high.

◆·◆·◆

When Marty's father said we would be going to a nice meal at the top of the Space Needle, I was nervous. Back East, I loved going to the Ponderosa buffet on Sundays for salad and a baked potato. On special occasions, we went to the Patio Restaurant in the basement of the Hess's department store. Women walked through modeling the furs from the fifth floor, throaty voices telling us that we can purchase this coat for $1,135. On a kid's birthday, the waitress brought out the meal on a metal stove as a special treat. Their strawberry pie challenged the PP&L building for the title of tallest thing in Allentown. I hadn't been raised in a world where fork placement and order of spoons mattered, and I feared that Marty's family, the waiters and the other diners would all see through me for what I felt I was, an identity that embarrassed me: a Pennsylvania Dutch girl who didn't know about the things that seemed important to the rest of the world.

I wore a forest green Limited Express shirt with navy blue pants, the fanciest clothes I owned. We sat in the dining room, and I watched the view as we spun. I was thankful for the slow pace. I read the menu and didn't recognize much of the food, but I saw lobster and knew that it was fancy. Lobster stuffed with chicken. I went for it, thinking my order might class me up a bit. It was the first and the last time I ate lobster, as I became a vegetarian soon after my trip.

———◆◆◆◆———

Marty's family wasn't wealthy. They were kind people who wanted to make sure that I had a great time while seeing their son. When I left, I knew that I wouldn't see Marty again, and while I was sad, I was okay with that knowledge. I was leaving as a more confident young woman, one who would no longer have a problem getting on a plane by herself or navigating a new social situation. In some ways, Marty's leaving was the best thing that happened to my young self. I know it is only a matter of time before Washington takes another person I love.

Learning by Wandering

SEATTLE

By Sue Kreke Rumbaugh

As we neared Seattle, I raised the window shade to take a look, but the sun's rays were so bright, I had to lower it immediately. In the fraction of a second that I was able to capture a glimpse, I saw a blanket of clouds. Most likely the people below us are getting rained on, I thought.

The cloud cover from our vantage point was beautiful, as though an ocean of cotton-ball tufts stretching out as far as I could see. I imagined the belly of our plane brushing over their irregular mounds, dunes of water and wind. I closed my eyes and drifted into thought, replaying the image of white puffy clouds against a deep blue sky. I tried imagining what our trip might bring.

Adjusting a small pillow propped against the window, I took in a deep breath and hoped to slip back into sleep before landing. I listened to the whirr of the engines and rocked with the plane's glide that filled me with a rush of joy for all that might be possible.

Soon, the crackling noise of the intercom startled me awake again. A pilot's voice announced that it was time to prepare for landing. I sat up, put on my sunglasses and slid open the shade again to study the white clouds. This time, I saw something unusual. I leaned forward to get a better look, bumping my head against the Plexiglas window.

At first I wasn't sure, but then I could see that it was definitely a mountain. It has to be Rainier, I thought. My eyes still wanted sleep, and I worked to focus on the ice-covered rock that poked through the clouds. It was magnificent. The bottom of the snowy peak was dressed in a skirt of cloud tuffs that clung to its sides. Slowly, I watched as the shades of color appeared:

white and beige, black and blue-gray. It looked out of place, this pyramid in the sky.

My introduction to Mount Rainier, Seattle's nature signature, caught me by surprise. Its peak, which appeared suddenly, disappeared just as quickly. This would not be the last time we would struggle to see it.

It was June 2011, weeks after I finished teaching and giving my last examination for the semester, when we soared through the sky from the East to West Coast to explore the great Northwest. Just days into a one-semester sabbatical leave from my university, I was ready to relax. I was also ready to discover what this region had to teach me.

We landed and took a cab to our hotel in the city via a stretch of elevated highway that ran alongside the blue waters of Puget Sound. When we turned right, suddenly the nose of our cab pointed into the sky, the engine roared and I felt the strain of the car as it labored to transport us up this steep hill, a foothill of Mount Rainier.

Finally we arrived at the Sorrento Hotel in a quaint neighborhood near the center of town. The setting is ideal in that it is tucked away yet close to everything, including the Seattle Public Library that we had been advised to tour. With eleven floors and more than one million books, its location on the side of the hill provides dramatic views of the city. Its design, however, keeps one's interest focused inside.

The tour is worth the trip. Starting at the top, we worked our way down varying sets of stairs and escalators that weave in and around bookshelves, walked down ramps that lead through doorways into rooms of glass and art. Each floor brought with it a new theme, new light and color. Dutch architect Rem Koolhaas's work displays imagination as well as humor. His fourth-floor design, a red circular corridor opening to neutral conference rooms, is easily a favorite.

In addition to being close to the library, this Seattle neighborhood has additional interesting architecture—old and new mix for a taste of the city's rich history and willingness to embrace change. The only thing missing for me was a view of the fourteen-thousand-foot-tall Mount Rainier.

The following day we toured the city, walking down and back up the steep slopes to our hotel. Below, in the city center, we acted as the consummate tourists: stopping in stores and restaurants, buying gifts and trinkets for family and friends as well as ourselves, to remember these few days we spent in this young, lively and diverse city.

We found our way to Pike Place Market, which appears in all of the marketing materials, and joined the crowd gathered around its famous fish market to watch the animated workers. These salespeople didn't just stack, prepare and sell fresh seafood in the market: they matched fish with owners. Creatively, they mingled in the crowd, escorted passersby to the cases of ice filled with seafood looking for a new home. They held up fish for customers' inspection, chanted songs using fish as puppets and tossed the creatures back and forth to attract and entertain potential customers.

We played along with the fish matchmakers' antics for a while, until we were introduced to a two-foot-long fish named "Baby" that was "perfect for our dinner table," according to one of the specially hired and carefully trained fishmongers. We explained that it was not our lack of interest in Baby's bright eyes and pouty lips—it was our lack of a kitchen that led to our denying her. With our rejection, he clicked his heels, bowed his head and turned to the couple across the floor who had observed the whole routine. Baby was quickly adopted. Within minutes we shuffled out the door through a sea of people and were on our way to our next tourist attraction, the Space Needle.

We walked quickly, map in hand. Not liking to be a typical tourist, I grumbled at our fast pace, wishing we could discover this place slowly and away from the crowds. This was not possible, however. More than nine million people visit Seattle each year. So, since I wanted to see and experience this tower in the sky, a centerpiece of the 1962 World's Fair, I braved the crowd.

Soon I found myself standing in line with my irritable tourist syndrome kicking in. I couldn't help but think of salmon swimming upstream as we passed tourists as eager as we were to see the view. When we finally reached the elevator, I felt relief. Then I was quickly agitated again, feeling like a sardine packed tightly in a tin can.

When we reached the top, I forgot about the crowds and my disdain for slogging around as a tourist. All of Seattle, the Puget Sound, the peninsula and the islands that make up this community stretched out before us. After walking the rim and wanting to gaze for a while longer, we decided to continue our touristic adventure and sit down for lunch in the famous revolving restaurant. Although impressed, it was not my first time in such a moving feast establishment. My hometown of Pittsburgh, Pennsylvania, had one for years. But when our name was called, I was delighted. We took our seats and prepared to order wine—from Washington State, of course. The sommelier, however, had a different idea. He liked our last name and suggested Rombauer Chardonnay, from Sonoma, California, instead. In our allotted time, we enjoyed our meal, our wine and the grand view. That is, without seeing Mount Rainier, this city's iconic but fickle rock formation.

"It's right behind the puff of clouds over there," our waiter said, pointing off in the distance to a wall of clouds. He added, "She may not come out for us today." And I believed him. "I've been here ten years and have seen her maybe only three times," he added.

With this information, I now wanted to see the mountain even more. It became of prime importance. I wondered if I could be satisfied with our trip if it turned out that we did not see it.

The following day, we diverted our attention from this pending disaster by planning and undertaking other adventures, including exploring two local universities, one by foot and the other by cab. We began with Seattle University, a Jesuit-tradition university within walking distance of our hotel. As we walked through the campus, we discovered a variety of beautiful buildings, including a chapel dedicated to St. Ignatius designed to capture light at various times of day and fill the interior with seven varieties of color, serene, a quiet oasis in the city.

From here we wandered through the gardens and took in the scents and scenes of the wide variety of flowers, trees and shrubs, many of which I had never seen. One after another appeared, and we snaked through them before emerging into a courtyard. This open-air space features a water fountain that erupts with water spray upward. Its mist drifted over us and felt refreshing on this summer afternoon. We sat for awhile, resting perched on the low wall surrounding the unusual but lovely space. Here we watched the sun's rays slice through the university's buildings, illuminating the top of the water's flow in such a way that it glowed. The light in Seattle is different than the light in the east.

Because we were so taken by the beauty of Seattle University, we felt even more excited to see the University of Washington. With only a couple of hours of sunlight remaining, we were eager to arrive quickly, and so we ran to catch a cab. We wanted to be able to enjoy its botanical gardens and to possibly find a view of Mount Rainier. The university, after all, was supposed to have the best.

We wondered. We hoped. And finally we arrived on campus. We walked quickly through Red Square, to the Rainier Vista corridor, hoping to catch a view of the elusive stranger.

As we rounded the buildings on the square, it appeared. At the end of a long mall formed by university buildings stood Mount Rainier. It was clear, visible, glowing in the late-day sun—it was stunning. The University of Washington is indeed the perfect place to view this volcanic peak. Pink and blue, purple, orange, red, gray and white, the mountain stood bare and

Seattle University's garden.

bold in the evening's sun. Finally Mount Rainier had allowed us to see it. Just as glorious as in pictures, as spectacular as we had been told and more impressive than my imagination could muster, Mount Rainer is, after all, a "must see."

When our trip came to an end, we left the way we came, but I knew that something was different. Something inside me had changed. As our plane lifted off the ground and sped into the sky, I watched as we slid through

The view of Mount Rainier from the University of Washington's campus.

the clouds that would soon conceal Mount Rainier once again. I sat up to catch a final glimpse and stared at it for as long as I could. It was then that I realized the power of wandering—to experience the unexpected and to be changed by it. This is the key to learning, I thought. Then I sat back and settled into my seat, preparing for the five-hour plane ride home.

Glenco Gang

RENTON

By Stefeny Anderson

Community. That is what I had as a child. Our neighborhood was like a small town within a smallish town. Glenco had been my home since the birth of my little brother. Everyone—and I mean everyone—knew one another's business, and it was okay because we all helped one another. For years, our house was the center of all summer activities since all the kids came to my mom's "day care." Mornings were spent sitting around our old oak table with all the leaves in it, the table littered with seven different types of cereal, a couple gallons of milk and some fruit. If able to, mom would put wheat germ on the cereal. She was like a ninja. We would have to eat it, too.

With all that togetherness, the kids of the neighborhood were tight. We were one another's entertainment. No cellphones or video games and very little TV. We played; we invented. Among one of our favorite games was "Spiderman versus Darth Vader," with an elaborate set of rules that changed daily but a great game of chase that we played all on our bikes. There were a few injuries, but no one died. One day, as I ran from "Darth Vader" by gaining speed down the big hill in our 'hood, I pedaled vigorously, looking back over my shoulder to make sure that my nemesis was not gaining on me. As I neared the end of the block, I took one last look back and in doing so missed the curb. I flipped through the air, landing flat on my back. Silence reigned at that moment. Everyone stopped. I got up, wiped the tears from my eyes and got back on my bike. There was no time for tears. We had important things to do.

Stefeny and her dad.

Being the only girl in the neighborhood, I played what the guys wanted or didn't play. My fancy Victorian dollhouse I received for my seventh birthday served as the Rebel base in their fight against the Decepticons. My one Barbie was the Amazon warrior goddess that fought for the good guys. We played football in the street, stopping only for the cars as they passed through the 'hood. In the summers, we stayed out until 11:00 p.m. playing Kick the Can or catch at the park. The cry of the Three Musketeers would describe our ethos perfectly: all for one, and one for all!

One normal Saturday morning, the mettle of our neighborhood character was tried. We were given a moment that would test all that we had learned in our years of chasing one another through the streets of Glenco. My brother and I sat in our pj's watching cartoons; Dad read the paper until the time he could watch basketball on TV. Mom cooked in the kitchen. From the driveway, all we heard was the sound of screeching tires, the pounding of feet and our door being flung open. A lady ran into our house screaming, "I need your phone!" This was much more interesting than the Snorks, so my brother and I turned our attention to her. Mom tried to get this unexpected houseguest to take a breath and explain what was happening. We got a broken story about how earlier that morning, her husband had left their truck running in front of their condo when he ran in to get something and someone had stolen the truck. At that very moment, her truck was parked on our street, and she saw two young men walking away from the truck into the "woods" behind our park.

Cartoons were forgotten. Mom called 911, while Dad got the lady a glass of water. My brother and I kept watch out the window. Others began to sense the events unfolding in the neighborhood because we saw curtains pulled away and doors opened so the neighbors could see what was happening at the Anderson house.

Suddenly, my brother and I saw two young guys walk out of the woods toward the truck. The woods to us were a magical place with two ponds, lots of tadpoles, frogs, snakes and adventures. When we got older, we learned that there were nefarious acts going on in our woods: drug dealing, a horror that our little eyes and mind were somehow shielded from. Upon the call to Dad that the guys were on the move, he jumped into our brown station wagon in his pj's and slippers and parked right next to the truck to wait as the boys walked the block to the scene of their crime. We stood on the porch and watched as Dad confronted the young men. He called them over to his car. As they walked over, Dad said something to them, and then they bolted and jumped a six-foot fence. The moment took us all by surprise. Dad got out of the car and stared at the fence the thieves had hurdled. The crowd in my house filed onto the front porch. The sirens came closer and closer. The excitement was too much for my brother and I to handle. We had to get involved with this adventure. When we saw the police cars turn onto our street, we turned and ran into the house.

My brother and I threw on clothes, grabbed our bikes and yelled for all our friends to join us. That was the method of communication back then: the call of the neighborhood. All the kids gathered at our house when the first cop car pulled up. It was mobbed by eight kids on bikes all wanting to tell their story. We were the only ones with the whole story, but Dad stepped in and let the officer know what had happened.

By this time, there were three police cars and six officers. The adults began to strategize about how to circle the neighborhood and capture the thieves. The children of the neighborhood soon saw that their plan was not going to work. We knew the shortcuts, the houses without fences where thieves could cut through the yard, the secret passageways. We were the keepers of the secrets, and we were ready to lead the chase. Needless to say, the officers were reluctant to be led by a group of young kids on bikes, but we didn't give them a chance to argue as we split into three groups and called for the police officers to follow us.

The music of the great chase scenes played in our heads as we divided the neighborhood. Our screams could be heard throughout: "They cut through the alley!" "They are headed to the Miller's yard, go up the hill and cut them off!" The adrenaline pumped. Our bikes were not stealthy, as most of us had baseball cards in the spokes, but it didn't matter. The gang was a well-oiled machine with a profound knowledge of the area and an overwhelming desire to get the bad guys. Every movie we had ever seen was flashing in our eyes. Then, just like that, it was over. With our "expert" knowledge of the lay of the land, the police captured the culprits in twenty minutes.

As the thieves were taken away in a police car, we gathered in front of my house once again. The officers gave us their thanks in the form of Seahawks playing cards that we placed on our chests to show our honor. Though we all had a different version of what happened, we could all agree on one thing: it was a great adventure.

Baby Luke's Daah *of the Natural World*

TACOMA

By Kase Johnstun

My one-year-old son, Lukas, has not broken the talking barrier yet. He is not the genius child that our friends brag about, the Einstein child who started to string together sentences before he hit his first birthday, but he can *bah bah bah* with the best of them, inflecting high *bah bahs* and low *bah bahs* into his speech to express an opinion or comment on something Mary or I said. He likes to shout out *mmmhah* from his car seat to let us know that he's still back there and would like to tell us about the silly thing one of his buddies did at day care that day. We shout back *huhs* and *what's* and *are you serious*es to let him know we're buying what he's selling. He'll continue chanting until he either falls asleep or we get where we are heading.

He can say *mama* and *dada*, but before he said those clearly, he said *tita* in honor of our chocolate Labrador named Tica, the love of his young life, which he follows onto her floor pillow and snuggles up against like a nursing puppy. We know what he's talking about when he uses these words.

When Lukas sees something new, something amazing or baffling or an animal that does not belong to us—a squirrel, a bunny, a hummingbird—he extends his right arm out in front of him, and at the end of that arm he closes all his fingers except for his pointer and whispers just loudly enough for us to hear him, "Daah," which sounds closest to *thaaat*, as if he's saying in an amazed whisper, "Oh my gosh, look at *daah*." If he sees a bee, he points and says, "Daah"; an elephant at the zoo, "Daah"; a budding rose, "Daah"; or a flash of lightning that pops in the night sky outside our window, "Daah." The theory that he *only* busts out *Daah* to express delight in something new in his budding world has been tested in our front yard, at the zoo, in the rose garden of our local park and, most recently, in the rare, non-tropical rainforest that sits at the base of Mount Rainier.

I grew up in the foothills of the Rocky Mountains, climbing the sagebrush-covered faces of the Wasatch Front in Ogden, Utah. Long before developments covered the Uintah Valley, a mile of cattle fields stretched from our backyard to the white rapids and mellow pools of the Weber River. From our front yard, my brother and I set out on day-long journeys to climb up and up and up until we stood nearly parallel to the steep mountain face and the angle of the slope stopped us from climbing any higher. Those days living from river to cliff made me an outsider, not the Ralph Macchio or Charlie Sheen type of outsider, but a person who looks up at the sky, and if there is any hint of blue in it, I'd rather be outside, running, hiking, cycling, even mowing the lawn.

Mary and I moved to Tacoma, Washington, in February 2008 and found that full-blue skies during nine months of the year are as rare as blue diamonds. When the layer of overcast followed the Cascades southward and we woke to sunshine one Saturday morning, I knew that my little family could not spend the day indoors, so we packed up all the necessities that accompany a one-year-old boy—diaper bags, snacks, one off-road and one casual stroller, little jackets and miniature Converse All-Stars that make me giggle when I see them—and drove west to the Carbon River Entrance to Mount Rainier National Park and the rare, non-tropical rain forest that lies at its feet.

Luke *mmmhahed* for a few minutes after we pulled our tiny car out of our driveway. But he fell fast asleep and stayed that way through the tiny cities that we passed through, cities sprinkled like crumbs to lead us home along the asphalt path on the way to the big volcano. He slept through the twists and turns of the snake-like road that weaved its way through fields, at first, and then into the heart of a body of seventy-five-foot-tall pines. He woke minutes before we pulled into the parking lot outside the ranger station and told us he wanted out with his newly acquired ability to mimic crying.

Parking the car at the end of a line of cars on the road, the overflow from the eight-spot ranger station parking lot, I jumped out of my seat, opened Luke's door and grabbed the little guy from his car seat. The second his face pushed into the canyon's breath, a smile moved his pouty lips upward, and within a second, he spotted the flowing Carbon River behind me and let out a reverent *Daah*. Mary pulled his off-road stroller from the trunk and attempted to strap him into it for a couple-mile walk along the river's

Kase and family.

growing and shrinking edge, but the moment she placed him into the seat, his upturned lips turned downward and the fake cry resurrected into the moist rainforest air. Instead of a long walk along the river with the boy in the stroller, we stood at the beginning of the .3-mile trail loop for kids, one that I would have never allowed myself to take in the past.

With Luke in my arms and Mary following with the camera, I walked onto the wooden path that stretched out into the rainforest. Luke wobbled with each step, but his eyes remained focused on the rich, dark greens of the forest and the dark, rain-saturated browns of the tree trunks that climbed so high into the sky we had to lean backward to find their tops. When Luke noticed the slightest movement in the landscape—a drifting leaf on the surface of a long pool of water, the flap of bird's wings, the shift of a branch from the weight of dropping moss, the spreading ripples from a drop of rain—his head turned to find the sound, his arm shot out forward and his finger pointed toward the movement, all actions serving as a fanfare for a quiet, holy *Daah*. We walked slowly over the boarded path and took family-self-shots on the camera, but Luke, usually a ham for the camera, did not look toward it once. We have twenty shots from that day, and in every one, Luke looks out into the lush, new world around him; his lips are parted saying *Daah*, and his eyes spread wider for the forest's music than for any bunny that he had seen in our yard.

We fed him a distracted lunch by the white caps of the Carbon River rapids. We eventually put him back into his car seat, and the moment he was strapped in, the reverent quiet that had possessed him for the last couple hours disappeared, as if telling his toys all about his experience.

Who We Really Are

TACOMA

By Julie Hall

F rom my great-grandfather's arrival in Tacoma on his twentieth birthday in 1881 to Girl Scout camping adventures in the 1930s, to great-aunts with beehive hairdos and horn-rimmed glasses to hand-tinted baby portraits, the thing I love the most when I visit my grandmothers is listening to the stories of their childhoods and family legends.

When I hear stories of my Grandmother Anne's love for music and playing in the Tacoma Philharmonic in the 1940s or of my Grandma Donna meeting my grandpa at the roller-skating rink, I hear my own story.

Anne

As we sit in her tiny living room, my Grandmother Anne—we call her Grammo—slowly turns the thick black pages of a photo album filled with small, faded black-and-white pictures dating back to the early 1920s, when she was a baby. I called her before my visit to ask if we could look at old photos together as I hadn't seen many photos of her early years. Grammo has never been one to volunteer her story. But as we go through these photos, I find her to be open and candid as she shares early memories of her unique life in Tacoma on the cusp of the Great Depression.

The beautiful nineteenth-century house and sprawling gardens took up a quarter of a city block in North Tacoma. Up on the roof five stories high was a widow's walk that provided a nice place to enjoy an impressive panoramic view of Commencement Bay. It was a formal home, filled with servants, fine furniture, Persian rugs, tapestries, statues, silver and shelves stuffed with books. Grand dinner parties were hosted around the great mahogany dining room table, and sometimes there were dances in the big hall. The rugs would be rolled back and the room filled with men in their tuxedoes and women in their long evening gowns. They would dance into the night to records played on the old Victrola.

Meanwhile, upstairs in the nursery that took up much of the second floor, three little girls ate their dinner with their governess. Theirs would be from a separate menu and was hoisted up from the kitchen by means of a dumbwaiter. Lunch was the only meal they shared with their parents. The youngest of the three girls was my Grandmother Anne.

Anne was born in that big old house in North Tacoma in 1921. Her father was a prominent businessman and leader in the community. He was twice the age of her mother and old enough to be the girls' grandfather when they were born. When he wasn't traveling for long periods of time to Europe and to the Orient, he was busy with his many business ventures. Anne's mother, the daughter of a minister, was raised in a strict and rigid environment where she learned to be a woman of duty. For her this meant a respectable place in society, hosting grand parties and supporting local charities. She also saw to it that her spirited young daughters were being raised to become proper little ladies by sending them to the best schools where they might make friends with children from "good" families. Anne was a shy and quiet girl with loud thoughts. Her sensitivity caused her to try to please and to keep up with the demands of her young life, but as she struggled, she was slowly being shaped into something very different than her mother had hoped for.

Grammo and I take a break from the photo albums to eat a simple lunch at the round table nestled in a breakfast nook in her kitchen. As we eat, she talks to me like a contemporary and tells more stories about my family that cause the bits and pieces of the family legends I was told when I was young to come together and connect, shedding new light. After lunch, I wash up the dishes, and Grammo asks if I want dessert. She pulls Oreos out of the freezer with a sheepish little grin. We always have frozen Oreos at Grammo's.

When Anne's parents were married, her father already had a grown daughter who was just a few months older than his new wife, which caused some tension between the two women. Anne's mother had known only a simple and modest life, so as the young new bride of this important and wealthy man in Tacoma's elite society, she was determined to live up to the challenge of becoming worthy of her husband and his daughter. Even though the two women warmed up to each other eventually, Anne's mother, who thought it seemed everything came so easy to her stepdaughter, was forever in competition with her.

Although Anne's father had sold most of his stocks before the Depression hit, he did lose enough money and property that he was forced to make adjustments for his family. He traded some real estate with a man who owed him money and in return acquired the man's newly built home on Gravelly Lake in Lakewood. Anne's family left their home in the city and moved to the country.

Their new life in the country meant the family was no longer able to employ a household of servants. However, unlike most families at the time, they were able to keep a maid, a cook and a driver who was also known to care for the gardens. Though the country house was much smaller than their city home, it was still beautiful and grand and was situated on five acres overlooking the lake. Another quality that appealed to Anne's father was that his adult daughter would be their neighbor, with only a field separating the two houses.

Life as they knew it slowed down, so Anne and her sisters began seeing more of their mother and of their father, who was getting older as he neared retirement. They didn't know as many people in the country, so instead of hosting elaborate parties five to six nights a week, they had family meals every night. Their social life consisted of hosting Anne's half sister and her husband, who would come over from next door once a week for dinner and a game of bridge.

Though they spent more time together as a family when they moved to the country, there was still a formal and distant way of relating between them. Anne often felt like she was living in a boardinghouse. Meanwhile, their city home sat empty for years; when it suffered a burst pipe that flooded it, the house was beyond repair. The grand house of luxury and abundance sat abandoned and in ruins, and eventually it had to be torn down.

Grammo and I go back into the living room and she puts a CD in the player. It's Beethoven's 7th Symphony, Mvt. II.

When they lived in the city, Anne and her sisters attended the prestigious Annie Wright Seminary, where in the second grade Anne was one of two students in the class. Anne struggled in school during those early years. When her family moved to the country, she was enrolled in Park Lodge Elementary, a coed public school where the class sizes were much larger and the academic expectations more rigorous. Although it was certainly an adjustment, she began to conform. She got to know children who weren't only from upper-class families, and she felt she could identify with these real, ordinary people. She felt as if she were let out of prison and began to come out of her shell, becoming involved in school activities and joining clubs. But Anne began to feel the weight of being from a wealthy family who experienced such abundance while her friends suffered so much want. She felt ashamed. She wouldn't even invite a friend to her house; until she got to know her as a person, Anne wouldn't dare let them see where she lived.

Anne and her sisters were rebellious, enjoying the new freedoms they experienced in going to public school. While her sisters rebelled by sneaking out with boys and going to parties, Anne's big rebellion was against her mother's Presbyterian beliefs. When Anne enrolled at the Helen Bush School in Seattle, it was required of all the girls to attend church on Sunday. Anne started sneaking to Mass, which infuriated her mother, who ordered the school's headmistress to see to it that Anne was not to even speak to a Catholic without the presence of a chaperone.

Anne did well at the Bush School and excelled in music. She had dreams of attending Julliard, but after studying abroad in France for a summer, her flute teacher recommended she go to Eastman School of Music instead. Anne graduated from Eastman with her bachelor's degree in music, but because there was a war on, she switched her focus to begin a degree in nursing. She worked as a nurse for a pediatrician back home in Tacoma thereafter, where she worked until she married my grandfather in 1951.

After raising her family, Anne went back to school at Seattle University in the mid-1970s, where she studied pastoral ministry. After working for years caring for people in her parish church, she felt she could never fully retire and continued to volunteer for St. Vincent De Paul's, to help people in need by just making herself available. Even now, at ninety-one, she visits "the lonely and the sick" daily in her new home at an assisted living facility.

We talk a little longer, this time about me and my little family. She listens and empathizes and offers words of encouragement and wisdom, which I treasure. But by now it's getting late, and it's time for me to go home. When we hug goodbye, she thanks me for coming and for listening. She says telling these stories feels like she took a trip back in time.

Anne in the garden outside her home in Tacoma, Washington, in 1925.

Donna

Visiting my Grandma Donna and Grandpa Herb during the winter months brings everyone indoors for a change because their beautiful garden, the beach, the boat and the lake are either frozen or getting soaked in rain. Without the diversions of the activities outside, we all sit in the tiny cabin-home and visit. I walk over to join my thirteen-year-old daughter when I see her admiring the contents of the china cabinet in the dining room. "What is that?" she asks, pointing to a mother-of-pearl ashtray. Grandma comes over and opens the glass cabinet doors so we can have a better look at what's inside, and she begins to explain each piece's origin and who gave it to her. She tells stories of her mother and of her grandmother, and we sit enraptured as more stories of her early life emerge.

Their voices could be heard from miles away as the laughter and cheerful shouting echoed across the lake. Barefoot and in hand-me-downs, the children pushed past their parents, who were burdened with all the picnic supplies, and tore down to the lake, where they stripped down and splashed in. The two boys raced out to the middle of the lake while splashing and dunking each other playfully. The older girl stayed back with her younger sister, making sure she didn't venture out too far. Donna, my other grandmother, was always taking care of someone.

When Donna was born in Tacoma in 1931, the Depression was already in full swing. Like so many, her father was a hard worker who struggled to find a steady job. The family of six never stayed in one house more than two or three years at a time. They always lived in small, modest houses with wood stoves for cooking and for heat. Sometimes they had electricity, though they never had an indoor toilet. Donna always shared a bed with her younger sister, and usually the two older boys would share a bed in another part of the house. Sometimes all four children would cram into one room. This way of life never bothered the children, regardless of their parents' stress. They looked at each move as an adventure and each new house as their home.

As the relentless drizzle continues to dot the usually glassy lake, inside the cabin we gather around as photo albums are brought up from the basement and spread out on the dining room table. Grandma sits down with my daughter and me, and now my sister and cousin join us as we flip through page after page of old photos. Grandma's memory is astounding as she tells us about the faces in the pictures, where they were and what they were doing, who they were and how they lived.

Both of my grandmothers were children of May-December marriages. Donna's father was twenty-five when he met her mother at fourteen. After secretly seeing each other for a little over a year, they decided they wanted to marry. But as her parents refused them permission, they secretly eloped, hiding out in a little cabin on Patterson Lake. They stayed there only a few days before the police found them and took Donna's mother home. Since they were already married, her parents figured it was too late to fight it and decided to accept the situation for what it was.

There was always food on the table at Donna's house, but sometimes they wouldn't know where the food would come from until the eleventh hour.

Donna's sister remembers a time when, for some reason, they had a surplus of onions, so most of their meals were so full of onions they began to make her sick. It was a long time before she was able to eat them again.

Family legend has it that one afternoon some friends dropped by, and there was nothing in the house to offer them. One of Donna's brothers was playing outside with the other kids and found a nickel in a pile of dog poop on the sidewalk. He came running in the house with his treasure, proudly showing everyone what he found. Donna's parents looked at each other and shrugged their shoulders. They had the boy wash the nickel and run down to the corner bakery to buy a dozen doughnuts to share.

Donna's father took whatever job he could find and worked until he got laid off and had to set out looking for work once again. At one point, at the beginning of World War II, things were getting desperate, leaving Donna's mother at her wit's end. Like so many others during this time, she wrote a letter to Eleanor Roosevelt, telling her of their desperate situation trying and failing to find work to make enough money to feed the family. Mrs. Roosevelt responded by writing a letter to a contact she had in nearby Lakewood who arranged a job for Donna's father at a shingle mill on the waterfront in Tacoma. He worked for that company as a millwright until it closed, but by then he was ready to retire.

We sit and listen and ask questions as Grandma remembers. Every now and again, Grandpa pipes ups from his chair in the living room to correct Grandma's facts or to interject a memory or two of his own. I see Grandma watching Grandpa as he tells one of his stories, her eyes sparkling. She leans into me and whispers, "He always tells me this story. Sometimes we lie in bed at night and remember together and just laugh and laugh."

It's getting late, and the mouthwatering smell of the roast in the oven fills the entire house. Grandpa gets up from his chair and announces it's time to clear the table; dinner's almost ready, and he's starvin' to death. Grandma keeps talking as she walks into the kitchen to help get the rest of dinner ready as we pile the albums up to take them back downstairs until next time.

Donna's schooling was scattered here and there. They even moved down to California for a year when Donna was in the first grade while her father worked in a cannery. She and her brothers and sister attended four or five different grade schools.

Donna left school after the eighth grade. She went home for the summer and never returned. She kept busy working as a nanny for a family with a newborn. She bonded with this baby and learned how to take care of children and a house. She loved the work. When she was sixteen, she met a

Donna and her new husband, Herb, in Tacoma, Washington, in 1948.

handsome young man at the roller-skating rink. They met in October and married in March.

As we helped set the table for dinner, Grandma says to me, "I never had no regrets. I couldn't have got a better guy than Herb. I really couldn't have."

———•••••———

Eleanor Roosevelt once said, "I think that somehow we learn who we really are and then live with that decision." I see this in my grandmothers' lives. Their experiences, the places they traveled, the people they knew and loved, the books they read and the events in history they lived to see have shaped who they have become and trickled down to touch the generations that follow them.

Bumper Sticker Philosophy

Olympia

By Matthew Jaron

I live at the very southernmost reaches of the Puget Sound in Olympia, Washington. It is the capital of the state, due in part to its proximity to navigable saltwater and a waterfall that has provided hydropower to mills there since before the Civil War. Shipping, lumber and textile milling and fruit canning made fortunes in Olympia during the early part of the Industrial Revolution. Census data shows that until 1870, Olympia had a larger population than Seattle. But by the turn of the twentieth century, the Northern Pacific Railroad had bypassed Olympia in favor of Tacoma in what must have been a terrible blow to the economic hopes of the merchants and city fathers of the time. But having been shut out as a shipping hub then could not have worked out better for us today. We got to be the capital but never got to be a big city. Never really boomed, never really busted. The young and single do not often stay long amongst us, favoring the glamour of the Emerald City to our north, the folky night life of the Rose City to our south or the promise of warmth and sun in California. But that only ensures that we stay small and quiet and full of families unafraid to have their kids walk or bike to school. We have settled quite comfortably into a certain, if not anonymity, then a benign absence of attention.

In some ways that anonymity makes us Olympians the perfect microcosm of the northwest region as a whole. With the exception of fans of professional and Division One college sports, who resent the East Coast bias in television coverage and consideration for the various MVP awards, northwesterners are generally at ease with having been more or less disregarded, ignored and left alone by the rest of the nation. Some of our neighbors in Oregon have even organized a negative propaganda campaign to remind the nation—especially their wealthy California neighbors—just how wet and slug-filled their inexpensive and beautiful part of the country is. If a little bit of constant rain is enough to keep us green and isolated, so much the better. Thus it is with some surprise that we have received a flurry of media attention here in what even the natives affectionately refer to as "the other Washington" for some recent landmark decisions about the legalization of gay marriage and the legalization of marijuana. We are as surprised to find ourselves in the national spotlight as the rest of the country is to find that anyone is actually living here. Outsiders, catching sight of us on the news, might wonder if we are *so* surprised by the presence of news cameras that we have forgotten to shower in the weeks leading up to the one brief, small, public demonstration of marijuana consumption that received worldwide publicity.

I know how it looks. The first word that flashes through someone's mind when they think of the Northwest (if they have any impression of us at all) is "hippies." At least that sums up the impression I had when I moved here eight years ago. I am a transplant here, one without longstanding in the community, without any particular expertise in its history and certainly without ambition to become one of the community's leaders, but I have come to love this place and do not picture ever leaving it. Certainly not for long. I came here with the expectation that nearly everyone I met would be some degree of latte-drinking, tree-hugging liberal who drove a Volkswagen Westphalia with two kayaks and three bikes strapped to the roof and bumper stickers that read, "I'm already against the next war" and "If you see this vehicle parked at Walmart, report it stolen." This didn't feel like an unfair judgment at the time, because I was excited about it. I consider myself a progressive and an environmentalist and presumed rightly that in moving to Washington I would be surrounded by more people of that sort. I was not convinced, however, that I would, or even really could, personally adapt to what I thought of as a "hippie" way of life. As much as I admired free spirits and lovers of nature and generally abhorred mall-based consumerism, I didn't think I could pull off dreadlocks, let alone drink soymilk or restrict my movie watching to subtitled documentaries. I certainly couldn't read any more New Age philosophy than fit on a bumper sticker. Besides, I had no cause to imagine the locals would accept me, a meat-eating square.

My previous experiments in self-transplantation taught me not to expect the open arms of welcome in any community; observation of a group of people, even living amongst them, should not be confused with membership. I have lived a decade or more in some places without ever feeling like I could rightly claim to be from there. I thought living among the Olympians would prove to be no exception, until I found I had gradually become one of them myself without even noticing. I had initially feared, or at least subconsciously guarded against, the idea of turning into an Olympia hippie. I was imagining that there would be some awful induction ceremony, first a tattoo of the recycling symbol, followed by a drum circle and a prayer circle and a meditation ring and a hoop of unity, or worse, that there would be some road to Damascus–style, blinding-light conversion experience that would instantly transform me, leaving me covered in ill-fitting vintage clothes, ranting about how the Ferret Rights Action Coalition is too political these days and how it used to really be about the ferrets, man. But that day just never came.

For me, being *from* Olympia came about by virtue of a sort of negative proof. The summer of 2012, I went back to my hometown in southeastern Pennsylvania for a wedding. I had not been back in years and was expecting a flood of memories to wash over me at every corner, but instead I found I couldn't find my way around anymore, certainly not on the back roads, roads on which I once knew every curve, dip and pothole. When intuition fails, memory misgives, and the old landmarks are tumbled or, worse, repurposed as something cleaner or brighter; when I have to humble myself and ask the woman's voice on my telephone to map a route for me, especially after the rude things I've said to her about how unhelpful and pointless she is; when I am plainly lost in the trees in a place that I think of myself as being *from*, it's probably time to admit I am not from there anymore.

Still, it feels as awkward to me to write "we" in referring to Olympians or Washingtonians or northwesterners as it does to say I have "read" a book when I really just listened to a recording of someone else reading it while I drove back and forth from work. I'm not sure I've earned the title. But if I ever worried that I might really turn into a hippie, or that my old friends back east might joke about me organizing a yoga-in for PETA or leaving teaching to sell wooden sasquatch sculptures from my website, I don't worry about it anymore. In fact, I cannot deny a growing sense within myself of something I had never known before: civic pride. I am living in the capital city of the most progressive state in the nation; it feels good to have played one person's part in leading the country in long-overdue decisions like marriage equality and the legalization of marijuana. Pride of place like that is unfamiliar to me and without precedent, but I can sure get used to it.

When I was growing up, the only people who would make a point of mentioning where they came from did not do so out of pride but rather in hopes of coming across as tough and hard for having been able to survive an upbringing there. No one I knew wanted to live where they grew up. It was not that they dreamed of other places being exotic. Ours was a homogenized culture with an increasingly metaphorical sense of place. We were the first of the pioneers in the digital age, the first to think of web addresses as places, the first to develop virtual versions of our personalities or, just as often, virtual versions of someone else's personality. Everywhere we go starts to feel the same as everywhere else. A sense of regionalism in speech or custom ceases to be a reliable marker of identity to us, let alone a source of pride. My generation's understanding of regionalism eventually boiled down to nothing more than a list of caricatures so passé that the ones that weren't racist weren't even generally offensive to anyone. And so where actual regional differences did in fact exist, we did not notice them or could not explain them.

This accounts for why in my late teens and early twenties I went around sweating in the heat and humidity of central Pennsylvania summer day after sweltering day, wearing a flannel shirt or tying it around my waist. I had no idea at the time why being cool had to mean being so hot. I just did it. I might have had some vague rationalization about doing my bit to obliterate fashion fascism, but in point of fact, I did it for the same reason that my friends' older sisters had pierced their ears with safety pins in the bathrooms of their parents' old farmhouses and did their eye makeup like Siouxsie Sioux. My favorite bands came from western Washington, so I wore what they wore, as did the thousands of sweaty college students I went to school with who *also* had never been to the Northwest. Here, actually *in* western Washington, there are few extremes of climate that would necessitate a real parka, but even summer nights are cold and damp enough to necessitate keeping a warm flannel handy. A flannel shirt is no goofy affectation. It also isn't some countercultural statement. It just makes sense. And if no one outside our little green corner understands the practicality and versatility of it, that doesn't make it any less sensible. That's just why the "far out, man!" stereotype misses the point.

Sure, we have plenty of what might elsewhere be perceived as tree-hugging spiritualism, not to mention some moralizing and self-righteousness about rights for humans, animals and plants, but that stems from a very practical sense of what is important to us, not just a deep, unbridled yearning to commune with ferns. There's a perfectly practical reason for our affinity with nature. We need more gear just to live here. In a half-day's drive, I can go from the beach to the snow avalanche zone. And we have what most people would think of as bad weather most of the time. If we already find ourselves prepared for adverse and changeable conditions, we don't have to be hindered by them, and we even learn to enjoy them. Of course, our behavior seems strange if one lives somewhere where rain can be avoided by simply waiting for the sun to come out. It's all a matter of perspective; my children who are natives here will surely think it strange that anyone might hang a line outside to dry their laundry.

For us, adaptability becomes a way of life. Where once I might have reflexively mocked "Friends don't let friends harm waterfowl habitat" and "Don't Eat Conflict Tomatoes" over the tailpipe of the Subaru wagon ahead of me, now I get it. In a place where people recognize that change is possible, they start to care about the direction of it. There is also something about living with an active volcano in our backyard that on a tectonic whim could blow its top off and drown our neighbors in mudslides eight stories deep that changes our relationship to change. It makes us feel like we should not prioritize our tradition over our condition and that sensible change should not take forever. We're ready for it, and whatever we are not ready for we can adjust to if need be. Putting up with more jokes about patchouli or masters degrees in Hacky Sack Studies turns out to be a small price to pay for getting to live in the most free and equal state in the whole union.

As a new citizen of Washington, at first I scoffed in disbelief at what turns out to be a remarkably effective mode of direct democracy not practiced in the East. I was shocked at first that Washington led the class of states that made smoking in public buildings illegal. I agreed with the decision, I just couldn't believe that such matters could be decided by referendum vote. How could we just change the law? What about the implications of enforcing the new law, not to mention the rights and responsibilities of business owners? But most importantly, how could we make a new law without the intervention of government representatives, first grandstanding in glittering generalities, then working out the details and then obfuscating them in unintelligible double speak? I felt something like what former Catholics must have felt during the Reformation, when suddenly they could no longer confess to a priest but had to talk to their Heavenly Father themselves. I thought it would never work. But it worked very well, indeed. It turned out that even people who were angry about the smoking ban generally respected and followed it.

Then a couple years later, we voted to allow physician-assisted suicide, and even though that was a vote that took a lot of reflection, we just did what seemed right and made it a law. The most important result of that historic decision is that nothing really happened. Most of the very small number of people who fit the qualification to get a lethal prescription, if they do get the dosage, only get it for peace of mind and rarely ingest it. The same seems to be happening with marriage equality and recreational marijuana. Mostly nothing. We had a flurry of lovely wedding ceremonies at the capitol building at Christmastime, and in Seattle, a few dozen people made a show of lighting up a few joints at midnight on the sixth of December, but it feels mostly like the law change is just a recognition of a long-standing status quo. No one seems to be coming forward with a lot of complaints. There has been no retribution, divine or federal. Sure there have been kinks. Figuring out the replacement language for "bride" and "groom" on the new state marriage licenses was harder than it sounds, but working out the will of the people is the business this town is in. And while much of the rest of the nation seems to still be figuring out how to recycle, or debating their levels of discomfort with public breastfeeding, we can't understand what is supposed to be so contentious about it. It might be that the insulating effect of living here amongst so many people of like mind has us confused.

But we're familiar with being a little bit disoriented. The weather prepares us for that as well. The fog often comes in here thick and low, so low sometimes that I walk out in the pre-dawn hours, and though I cannot see across the street, above is a crystal clear night sky made even brighter by the fog's having dampened the effects of the streetlight. And though I still have not lived here so long that I believe I can mystically augur my future from watching the stars, I have lived here long enough to cherish my present and any clear sky I can get. Perhaps the bumper sticker philosophy is wise after all: "Be Here Now."

Washington's Nuclear Disaster
ELMA

By Stephen Weiser

When most people in Washington think about nuclear disasters, the Hanford site probably springs to mind. Nasty stuff dating from World War II and the Cold War—radioactive, corrosive, poisonous. Piled in dumps, buried in corroded barrels, poured into wells—and now inching its way underground toward the Columbia.

But there was another one. It left no dead, no radioactive waste. It did leave two monuments on the Hanford Reservation and one on the rolling hills west of Elma. And for many, it left bitter memories of betrayal and financial loss. For me it left a set of arcane drawings—and recollections of touring a muddy construction site at the Satsop Nuclear Generating Station in the rolling green hills just west of Elma.

●━━●━━●

In 1957, a forward-thinking Washington state legislature created an agency to fund energy projects that would sell electricity to the public at cost—the Washington Public Power Supply System. WPPSS's first project, the Packwood Lake hydroelectric project south of Mount Rainer, began operating in 1964. As well as a financial success, it demonstrated that energy projects could have minimal impact on the visual and recreational environment.

In the 1970s, the agency embarked on an ambitious plan to secure the state's growing need for electricity. Nuclear energy was the popular solution then. Clean, efficient, no trainloads of coal, no massive coal piles on the front end, no dioxides, no mercury, no fly ash—it was thought by many to be the hallmark of progress and the harbinger of the future. WPPSS would build five nuclear generating stations, three at Hanford and two near Satsop.

Construction of the two Satsop stations was awarded to Morrison Knudsen Company in the late '70s. MK, a Fortune 500 engineering and construction company headquartered in Boise, Idaho, had been around since 1912, specializing in large, complex projects and innovative ways to complete them, most famously the first joint-venture created to build Hoover Dam. Its Power Group focused on energy facilities—coal-fired power plants, geothermal plants and refueling and decommissioning nuclear facilities.

The project was challenging. Power plants were largely unique in those days. Terrain, site conditions, fuel characteristics, water supplies, switchyard and transmission features were custom designs—hence costly. Environmental impacts had to be addressed—more cost. Fabrication had long lead-times requiring upfront capital. So it was important to get the plant on line as

Satsop construction aerial. *Courtesy of Satsop Business Park.*

soon as possible to begin recovering those costs. Thus, many such projects were fast-tracked—construction began before the final design was complete. The downside was the potential for delays if changes were required. While hydro and coal projects were known quantities, nuclear, with its new systems and configurations and stringent safety and oversight requirements, was not. Construction was already delayed by siting and environmental issues.

It was the kind of project Morrison Knudsen relished. Experienced engineers and construction personnel were assigned, transferred or hired. Jim, the project manager, was a rising star in the company—mid-thirties, a Rensselaer graduate, smart, savvy, self-assured. His staff was seasoned, drawn from successful (read: "profitable") projects. Subcontracts were put out to bid. People relocated to Elma. Locals hired on. Mobile homes outfitted as offices were hauled in. Trucks, scrapers, big cats, front-end loaders and backhoes appeared. Work began on site preparation. And "WPPSS 3&5" appeared on the project lists in the company's monthly magazine.

———◦•◦••◦———

I was with the MK Power Group's marketing section, providing technical communication support: writing proposals, presentations and marketing pieces; coordinating technical input, graphics and production; and assisting engineers in making direct, cogent and business-oriented presentations to nontechnical utility management personnel—including something for Jim's growing number of presentations. Because he *was* a Rensselaer graduate, most of his needs were for transparencies for an overhead projector, so my editorial duties fell to assisting those engineers who were *not* Rensselaer graduates.

One day, as I passed by our copy camera and darkroom, I saw that Sandy, our graphics designer, had hung up some prints to dry. They were strange, arresting, not like anything we usually produced—circles and what looked like spin-on oil filters all containing cryptic figures and letters. I studied the letters—they repeated, but without intuitive linkages. And the middle figures, if rotated, could have the letters in the same sequence as in the lower right figure—but then why weren't they rotated? Then there was I—floating on two figures? Three EL circles, but only one on the lower right figure. Did the top figure relate to the bottom? What is K? Emptiness?

Since we sometimes used the copy camera and darkroom facilities for personal work, I asked her if she were doing illustrations for some Freemason or Rosicrucian book. She laughed: they were plan drawings of the WPPSS containment buildings for a presentation Jim was giving. I was so struck by them I asked for a file copy—which I filed in my "interesting things" folder. I don't know if they were the final version—I never saw any of the word slides either, nor did I see the presentation. He probably didn't need to rehearse it.

Because we marketeers had no direct experience on construction projects but needed to know what we were marketing, we visited projects and talked to managers, engineers and workers. Jim and his wife lived in Boise, and since we socialized, it was natural that he invited me to the project. Shortly after, I was at a client meeting in Portland, so I rented a car and drove up I-5 to Elma. I had directions to the site but didn't really need them: the first cooling tower was nearly complete, rising up over the wooded hills south of Highway 12.

In his office, Jim introduced his staff—business manger, chief engineer, procurement manager, contract administrator, safety engineer and construction superintendent—and showed me blueline drawings, piping diagrams, photographs and the construction schedule taped to a wall with its critical path in red ink. He talked about the mesh of rebar inside the concrete walls, the barely fluid viscous cement that was so hard to work with, the continual quality control testing and the dread of design changes—they had just cut through the containment wall to reroute a redesigned pipe run. They would get labor and materials reimbursed by the change order, but the delay would impact the schedule.

Outside he led me through the second containment building along muddy walkways, through dank passages and under hoses dripping water—possibly to test my commitment to the three-piece suit and thin leather shoes that I was still wearing. He pointed out the vessel location and how it would be installed. I took photos to show our team, even though I knew that it was like photographing Chartres. We toured storage buildings filled with pipes and pumps, rebar, structural steel, electrical gear and spools of wire and cable. I took more pictures.

Back in Boise I showed the pictures and how they fit with Sandy's arcane drawings.

❖❖❖❖❖

Possibly the project was doomed from the start. Environmental issues delayed progress, design was complex and construction progress was hampered by changes. Costs increased, far beyond the estimates that the original bonds were based on. Published accounts report that the agency's management was inexperienced and thus unable to manage a project so large and complicated with its multiple sites, many contractors and differing designs. Already WPPSS had morphed into "Whoops!" in the media, and in our company's parlance as well: the moniker was too right.

Meanwhile, the nation suffered the Three Mile Island trauma, the China Syndrome fear film and a market turndown. Funding crashed. WPPSS defaulted on $2.25 billion worth of tax-free municipal bonds. Only one plant at Hanford was completed, the second mothballed and the third cancelled. The two units at Satsop were nearing completion, but work was nevertheless stopped. Mechanical and electrical equipment was salvaged out and the plants abandoned.

There was fallout—not radioactive, but still poisonous. Washington utilities—ratepayers—were on the hook for payback of defaulted bonds.

WPPSS changed its name to Energy Northwest in 1998. That has a better sound than "whoops."

Satsop Business Park. *Courtesy of Satsop Business Park.*

Recently, while downsizing my personal files, I came across the drawings. I wondered what had happened to the site, if it perhaps had a YouTube presence in the abandoned buildings section. While I found abandoned factories, abandoned power plants, abandoned towns even, there was no mention of Satsop. But GoogleEarth showed the site: it didn't look especially derelict. There were other structures nearby. Perhaps, I thought, it was now, like old missile silos, a dumpsite for hazardous waste. Further search revealed that it is not dead, not deserted, not a dump, but a thriving industrial and educational park. The cooling towers are still there, ghosts in the lush landscape, the containment and turbine buildings, too—unused, abandoned perhaps, but not forgotten.

How to Grow a Vigilante Garden

Longview

By Laura M. Gibson

Reaping

A few years ago, on a sunny spring morning, I woke up to find eight plants had been stolen from my front yard. Not whole pots of plants waiting to find homes, but mature bushes out of the ground. It took a couple beats to identify what was missing while I stood at my front window, eyeing the yard over the rim of a coffee cup, confused.

Once outside, I saw the story of their leaving. A trail of dirt faded off down the sidewalk two houses away and then veered into the street where the getaway vehicle had been parked. The thieves took a whole hedge of Pieris mountain fire. I liked them for their jaunty winter foliage, and they were one of the things I'd kept from the previous owners. Just at a place where I felt the yard had started to reflect my landscape sensibilities, I'd spent several weeks working on that section of the yard—taking down a hideous fence, planting native species. Now all I had was a bald section that looked like the front teeth of my yard had been knocked out.

My neighbor (I'll call him Tom) across the street had had some plants stolen the month before. The morning after it happened, several of us stood on the sidewalk in front of his house, shaking our heads at the news and wondering what the hell was going on in the world. Those were Japanese maples, still in pots sitting down the driveway and around the back of the house. Someone was paying attention. It was creepy. Tom bought more, and these got stolen too before he had a chance to put them in the ground.

The morning of our robbery, my husband, John, wandered out with the coffee pot to where I was sitting on the sidewalk. He stood next to me kicking at the dirt, cussing, one of his less acceptable mixed-company hobbies. He's actually kind of a poet. For pirates.

"What do we do? Call the police? Tom said all they did was take the details over the phone."

"I guess," John said. "Maybe they'll send someone now that it's happened three times." He pushed dirt into one of the holes with the toe of his shoe.

"Don't mess up the crime scene."

"This is shitty," he said. He topped off my coffee and went back inside.

It felt absurd to even suggest involving the police. I probably couldn't identify my plants. I doubted they'd be able to. It was the perfect crime, really. I looked around at my neighbors' yards from a lens of stealthy acquisition. Our street is a goldmine. Yard after painstaking yard is full of my neighbors' efforts at gardening. Our town, Longview, despite the passion of various groups to make it a place where folks want to move, is a struggling mill town. Its grid streets laid out with houses increasing in size are like a bar graph to show haves and have-nots. Of course someone wanted what I am lucky enough to cultivate.

Thirty minutes later, John and I stood on the sidewalk again with the police department's landscape crime detective (I'll call her Detective Blue). She was a one-woman show in a new position, created in response to a rash of landscape crimes, especially in our neighborhood. The fact that lots of other people were waking to find their yards pillaged made me feel only slightly better. Mostly, I had a hard time listening to Detective Blue while I mulled over the world's seedy underbelly of crimes undetectable.

Detective Blue wrote down all our particulars in her little notebook, licking her pen a few times to keep it working. She was from New Jersey. "We have a lead on a couple of plant rings in town," she said, "but I'm afraid your bushes are gone. How much were they worth?"

John threw the rest of his coffee onto the grass. "Oh, Jesus. Let me walk away first before she talks about how much she spends on the garden," he said.

"But those plants were already here," I said.

Detective Blue focused on her notepad, waiting it out.

"Also, you love the garden. Also, I get a lot of my plants from friends. It's environmentally friendly spending."

He shrugged. "I'm just saying let's not plant something else that's going to get stolen. It feels like lighting our money on fire."

"I can't just leave it."

Next to us Detective Blue opened her mouth to redirect us.

"Probably about $300," I said.

At that, John nodded as if this data validated all of his gardening arguments and said, "See? I can totally smell smoke."

As a gardener, I was out of whack for weeks. It was hard to reconcile what had been stolen. Not just plants, but sweat equity, creativity and joy. These particular plants weren't those I'd planted, but they represented something larger. I don't have ten acres (yet) to tend, and while I wait for the time when that works, I'm transforming the space I do have into something uniquely mine.

As a victim of theft, I was very pissed and a little paranoid. Someone had been casing the neighborhood. What else in my yard had the chance of being taken? Why hadn't the dog barked in the night? The windows were open. How could I not have heard someone digging, dragging and hauling outside?

I left that spot in the yard bare, afraid to plant the same thing and not sure what else to put there. Eventually I just seeded some grass in that spot, a remedy both John and I were happy about. And I spent a lot of time thinking about black market gardening and whether those chain-linked roadside stands that were stuffed with potted plants along the rural highways were legitimate.

A few months later, a zinger of an inspiration came while I was in the woods. There were *people* at the heart of those landscape crimes who were trying to eke out a living in a bad economy. What if those people were a bunch of kids? What if they lived off the grid? What would that look like? How would they decide what to steal? What native Pacific Northwest plants could they eat to survive? Who would be in charge? What else was at stake?

Thus began a novel in response to some of those questions. It's a mess. It's my first. The characters—all girls, a little band of thieves—are very patient with me, and we're searching for the story together. It might be a project that lives in a drawer later, and I'm not too romantic about it being a bestseller or anything. Some days it feels like giving birth. Not the fluffy after-labor-with-a-good-smelling-baby-in-your-arms part, but the in-labor-with-no-epidural part.

Still, I believe in the project as passionately as I believe in putting my hands in the dirt. I'm darn grateful for these girls in my life, which I guess means I'm grateful for being robbed, because without my gone plants I might never have pulled this collection of souls out of the "well of souls," as Dorothy Allison calls that place where inspiration is born.

Sowing

The view of my neighbor's house from my front window has pissed me off for years. It's a 1950s ranch, which is not its real problem. I've lived in a few ranches over the years and been happy—you can make them cute. But the offender on my current street is an unloved thing. Amidst a street of Craftsman and storybook homes built in the 1920s, it looks like it's crashing a Kentucky Derby party in a tight polyester pants suit. Beige asbestos siding, peeled country-blue shutter paint, cracked front steps and a tragic aluminum screened door that claps in the breeze. It's not good.

I don't know the owner, but I do know the house is a rental that can't seem to keep occupants for more than a few months. Two haphazard front garden beds of invasive plants have died, one by one, over the years. When someone comes to "care" for the yard, this means the high grass is mowed quickly and left to rot in clumps by a guy in a broken-down truck. The latest dead plant is tossed into the back of the truck on top of grass clippings.

Finally, about six months ago, there was nothing left in one bed but weeds and dirt. My next-door neighbor (I'll call her Sally) went over to weed it. The other bed, just beneath the living room window, was home to some jaundiced boxwoods. There wasn't much she could do with those.

The whole of this house, from its single-paned windows to its listing chimney and waist-high backyard grass, was asking for help.

The place has been empty this time for months, a "For Rent" sign advertising its awesomeness—"Great Neighborhood!"—at the edge of the yard. My neighbors and I hold our breath, hoping someone will move in soon.

Two weeks ago, the sky opened and delivered the gift of spectacular weather. A real, live bender. Since then, our street has been stoned out on Vitamin D and things in bloom. Every day I'd made an excuse to work outside in my own beds trimming and splitting plants.

A week into our sun blitz, I'd dug up several hostas and helliobores, intending to pot them up and donate them for our school plant sale. I pulled out the nandina (the owner before me had a real thing for plants from Asia). I set them out on the grass.

My plan was spontaneous. Mostly.

It was broad daylight. People were out mowing, raking, walking. I grabbed a shovel and a wheelbarrow and trundled my plants across the street. In front of the empty house, I set them out in a pattern I thought would work and planted them. I filled a watering can, added some fish emulsion and soaked them. After that, I sat on my front steps and had a beer, watching over my guerrilla garden.

The next day, one of my neighbors (I'll call her Dolores) said to me, "I *saw* you." Dolores wagged her eyebrows.

"Oh really? When?" (Uh oh. Trespassing is bad. I knew I should've done it at night.)

"I'm so *glad* you did *that*, because I was just about to do the same thing!"

Dolores brought over a holly bush from her yard. Another neighbor (I'll call her Martha) donated a Japanese maple. Tom mowed the grass. I mowed the grass twice when it got too high while Tom was away and then decided to pay my son to do it. More plants showed up mysteriously. I planted them all, and the place was really beginning to look like someone loved it, at least a little. We were cooking with gas. A community of garden lovers taking matters into our own hands! Next stop, a coat of paint! A new door! Re-pointing the chimney!

Today, I was working away at my desk, one eye on my new garden, thinking about when I'd get over there to water. (Hooking the hose up to their spigot was *definitely* goddamned trespassing, John informed me. Also, the water was turned off.)

Up pulled a beat-up pick-up, not the usual one. Out came a weed whacker. A man with a cigarette drooping from his mouth attacked the yard. My son had just mowed. Mr. Cigarette mowed again anyway. Then he took out the plants (Our plants! Sally's, Dolores's, Martha's and mine!) and threw them into a heap in the front yard.

I ran across the street, my hands in the air, demanding to know what his *plan* was.

He turned to look at me through goggles covered in wet grass flakes. "The guy's paying me to take all this out. He says they're dead."

I pulled a leaf off one of the helliobores and showed it to him. "Do they look dead to you?"

"Well. No." He looked over his shoulder at the boxwoods, already gone.

"Did someone buy the place? Or rent it?"

"I don't know, lady. I'm just getting paid by the owner to do the yard."

"Did he rent it? He never calls back." Even to my own ears I sounded pathetic.

"You want me to call him? I'll call him. Then I can get back to work." He dialed the phone, waited for an answer and fiddled with the handle of his weed whacker.

It's true I'd been calling the number every few days, pretending to be a renter. After the first few times, I called as *different* renters, leaving my home phone, or my cell, or John's cell number, which seems unhinged now that I have to explain myself. I'd just called again that morning as my real self.

"Um. Yeah. There's some lady here who's mad about the yard. She says she wants to talk to you." He passed me the phone.

"Oh, hiii. I live across the street." (Friendly. Check. Breezy. Check.) "You've got some guy here taking out all the plants? Because not all of them are dead, you know. (Oh dear. A little nasty.) I'm just hoping you aren't planning to leave the beds bare? Like they've been for, you know, a few years?"

Traffic noise on the other end. A siren flaring and fading. "I don't live in town, and it's hard to take care of it." A young guy. I'd heard he inherited the place from his mother.

"I bet."

Long pause. Another siren. "The last time I was there about a month ago everything was dead."

This was the time to tell him NOT ANYMORE. Garden vigilantism is your new friend, mister. But landscaping seemed a much bigger trespass than mowing. And I'd made rules about my methods, too, which suddenly seemed crazier than the fake identity calling. I didn't MOVE any plants already there. I just added them. I didn't sneak over at night; I gardened in the light of day.

"You've really let it go," I said. "Some of us in the neighborhood have been mowing the front grass."

He laughed. "Really?"

"Have you rented it out? Or are you selling it?"

"Oh, yeah. I've got a bunch of people looking at it."

This was a lie. I live right here, and no one has. I asked what the rent was, and he told me. His inflated figure explained why no one wanted it: he was smoking crack. He'd never get that kind of money for the place.

"Well, that seems like a lot."

Radio silence. Some honking and a woman shouting.

"Could you just not leave the gardens bare?"

"Yeah. Sure. Okay," he said, then hung up.

I asked Mr. Cigarette to save the plants he'd dug up and he said he would. "Could you put the boxwoods back in? They're pretty healthy, don't you think?"

"You gonna pay me?"

"You're already being paid, aren't you?"

"Just kidding. Never hurts to ask," he said and lit another cigarette. "I'm supposed to go to Fred Meyer and get new plants. You got a problem with that?"

Neighborhood
seed brigade.

He looked at me through the smoke.

I should've stepped away. Let well enough alone. Transferred my energies to another cause. "Can I write down some plants that would be good?" I said. "I mean, if it's all the same to you. If the owner doesn't care. It seems like he doesn't care."

"Knock yourself out, lady."

Even though I wanted to lurk around, making sure he'd be as good as his word, I didn't.

Later in the day, I checked to see what he'd done. The boxwoods had been replanted unevenly, like the person doing it was drunk. On the far end, the biggest one had its roots exposed and lay on the ground. Our plants, mine and Sally's and Dolores's and Martha's, were all gone.

I told myself I'd gotten what I deserved for muscling a situation that wasn't mine to steer.

Around nine in the evening my doorbell rang. Out front on the lawn stood Sally and Dolores. They were giggling, sharing a bottle of tequila hidden inside a paper bag.

"We don't know what the hell happened over there today," Sally said. She gestured to the house across the street. "Somebody told us they saw you in the front yard with that gardener guy trying to save the plants."

They laughed and offered me a drink.

"He said he'd save them for me," I said. "I guess he decided I was too insane."

"Come with us. We have a present for you."

They took me into Sally's backyard, where all our plants sat in a wheelbarrow by the garage.

"We got these out of the trash can behind that house," Dolores said. "Can you believe that asshole? Throwing away our plants?"

Sally took a swig of tequila and offered some to me. "We figured you'd want to...you know...*do* something with them."

Tequila's not my friend, so I said no to that. But I was up for gardening with my new posse anytime.

Mountains Beyond Mountains

Vancouver

By Jonathan Metz

My dim flashlight barely lit the emptiness in front of me. Complete silence, an ancient staleness to the cool air. Somehow, we had to get through an obstacle course made of only lava-rock, merciless on our hands groping through pitch-black darkness with nothing but instinct, faith and flashlights to guide us. I never really understood real darkness until I entered a cave.

The Ape Caves—ancient lava tubes in the Mount St. Helens wilderness carved into the landscape by an eruption two millennia ago. They had an ominous name, especially to a third grader. The only apes I'd seen were at the zoo or on TV and lived at large on the other side of the planet. The more terrifying but natural conclusion to a third grader: there must be apes that live around here, too.

An hour or so before, walking away from the parking lot toward the trailhead I asked Mom why they were called Ape Caves and hoped for a renewed confidence. I wondered if the person who named them mistakenly thought he was in the jungle or someplace with big, exotic primates. She laughed.

"Oh, no, there aren't any apes around here."

I sighed a great sigh of relief. "Good. So why are they called Ape Caves then?"

"They're called Ape Caves because there have been Bigfoot sightings around here."

I inhaled the fear back in my nose. My eyes darted from shadow to shadow between thick evergreen trees and moss-covered rocks, both plentiful along the side of the trail.

We came to the mouth of the caves—old lava-flows carved into the ground about two thousand years ago by Mount St. Helens—the great, white leviathan of southwest Washington. The beauty and the beast of our landscape.

"And...we're going...in *there?*"

We were about to spelunk around a deep, dark chasm for two miles in complete darkness where sasquatches could, waiting with their mouths wide open, devour unsuspecting day hikers. We had Kettle Chips with us. I thought if attacked, we could use the chips as a distraction to escape. But we'd have to give them the plain variety...there was no way I was going to give up the cheddar.

We descended the steps into the caves. I had to protect my mom and sister, Jonika, because by 1994 I was the man of the house at eight years old. I took the lead or the rear but never in between. I thoroughly swept the dark path in front of us with my flashlight. I occasionally flashed it behind us just to be sure we were alone.

I stood at the mouth of the cave and felt terrified to go in. Once in, however, my fear gave way to thrill. As we hiked through two miles of darkness, we followed the cave's twists and turns. We climbed through narrow passageways that gave way to big caverns. We climbed up and down rockslides and even scaled small cliffs. Finally, after what seemed like miles of hiking, we saw a bright light in the distance. We knew we had come to the end.

Though the journey was exciting, the fear that something might happen to us while we wandered these brooding, black chasms never left me. When we climbed up the constructed staircase toward the light and reentered the familiar landscape filled with lush evergreens and blue sky, it felt as if we had emerged from a long and difficult journey.

Even though I was only eight years old, I was aware of what the powerful message emerging from the cave symbolized. The longer I stayed in the cave, the more I desired to see the light again. And when I finally did, it was all the more satisfying. I felt satisfied not only because the fresh daylight felt good to my eyes, but also because I had endured a struggle. I also realized, though I may not have been able to put words to it, my emergence from the cave was symbolic of the growth I had just experienced.

It turns out, the caves were not named after monkeys or gorillas or "Bigfoots" of any kind but rather the members of an outdoor club who called themselves the St. Helens Apes. There had never been anything to be afraid of.

The memory of the caves also represents everything that a twenty-six-year-old still desires and is, in fact, still searching for.

Jonika and her mom, Judy, in the Mount St. Helens wilderness in the summer of 2005.

In 2012, I look back on my youth in and around my hometown of Vancouver, Washington. The Ape Caves, being one of my first outdoor hiking experiences in Washington, were just one of many unique backcountry activities that are afforded to Southwest Washingtonians. Residents of Vancouver and the Greater Portland metro area refer to the vast, endless Washington and Oregon backcountry as their "backyard." Locals are proud that the region sports a wealth of places to hike, camp, backpack, fish, ski, dirt bike, wind-sail and surf all within a few hours' drive. Growing up, I identified with that sense of regional pride that made me feel connected to my homeland, someplace important and unique. But even if such regional pride didn't exist, I loved the land I grew up in simply because it was my home, and I belonged there. The landmarks within and around Vancouver defined the shape of the community in which I lived and helped me identify with my home.

I spent my childhood exploring every surrounding road, building and natural land formation in all directions. After school, my best friend Justin and I would ride our bikes every place we could. We spent countless hours exploring southeast Vancouver, observing and memorizing street names, neighborhoods and district hubs as we went. When we first began our biking escapades in sixth or seventh grade, we explored surrounding neighborhoods I hadn't been to. As we graduated from elementary school, then from junior high and onto high school, we began meeting people from these neighborhoods. For me it was like putting a face to a name, and I felt I knew better the community I lived in. Later, when we both had our driver's licenses, we'd drive even farther than we'd biked in previous years and housesit for teachers who lived on the edge of town. Growing up, my world physically expanded. The map of my world, in my head, was always growing.

I wasn't satisfied, however, that my knowledge of the surrounding community ended with my hometown. I had to know what the greater region of Washington and the Northwest at large boasted.

Many times growing up I'd sit on the floor at the top of our stairwell where we kept on a bookshelf an old set of World Book Encyclopedias. The "W-X-Y-Z" volume was my favorite because it contained Washington State. I'd pore over maps of the Northwest terrain memorizing the names and locations of rivers, mountains and cities. Then, I'd test my knowledge by redrawing these maps from memory in Microsoft Paint.

Each time I explored a new place, I felt as I did when I explored Ape Caves as a kid. For me, it was one way that I fed my fix on adventure and mystery and exploring the unknown amidst the taxing journey of growing up.

There was one place, however, that symbolized my sense of place and my desire for new experience.

◆·•·◆

Mount St. Helens was once regarded as one of the most beautiful volcanoes in America before it incinerated one thousand feet from its previous elevation along with its entire north face in an unprecedented volcanic eruption in 1980. After such a devastating event—one that significantly impacted surrounding communities—it has slowly grown to become, again, one of the most beautiful landscapes in America. Its gaping crater rests under hundreds of feet of snow against the blanketed backdrop of pine trees—the telltale of Washington scenery.

Its eruption put our small region of the Northwest in the national limelight. More than any other feature in Southern Washington, Mount St. Helens—a scaling white monolith with a capped summit and smooth slopes—reminds me of the land I lived in and everything I loved about it. Perhaps that's why each trip to the mountain was meaningful.

Whenever my family and I went up to Mount St. Helens, we passed through a mass of green forest filled with infinite evergreens, throngs of Douglas fir, spruce and hemlock and log trucks ever-whizzing down the two-lane highway. During a family trip to the mountain in 1998, our final destination was the Johnson Ridge interpretive center. I was twelve. We had finally found a small scenic void in the great pine matter across from a ranger station. We went inside for maps, as we did every time we explored volcano country. The whole way there I was thinking, but wouldn't admit, "Is it...going to erupt while we're here today?"

I tried to reason with myself. "Probably not. It's been twenty-some years. That's a long time. It isn't likely it will choose today to erupt again."

A brief feeling of security, but then another thought, "Twenty years is a long time...maybe it's *due.*"

I couldn't shake the apprehension. "Have there been signs of activity recently?" Maybe the forest ranger behind the counter would know. I wasn't about to reveal my well-concealed fear, however. I devised with a clever way of inquiring about it. Maybe if I phrase the question the right way, the ranger may not think that *I'm* the one who is afraid.

"Do people ever ask if the mountain is going to blow while they're up there?" I asked the ranger.

"Oh, *all the time.*" She replied. And she went on to talk about how it was unlikely such an event would occur because there would probably be plenty of warning signs. I walked out with renewed confidence and felt rewarded for my wit.

Mount St. Helens reminded me that I didn't need to be afraid of the unknown.

—•◦•◦•—

In 1993, my family experienced its own eruption when my parents divorced. I was seven, and we lived in southeast Portland. After the divorce, Dad moved west to Beaverton and Mom to Vancouver. Jonika and I lived with Mom and had visitation rights to see Dad every other weekend and one night per week. Our lives felt unstable; I feared the unknown future ahead of us, one that did not include our parents being together.

Our biweekly travel to Dad's began with the hour-long trip back and forth from Vancouver to the suburbs west of Portland. Along the way, I memorized my landmarks. My street names. They became *my* hills, *my* buildings, *my* tunnels and *my* radio towers. Growing up in two different places and everywhere in between, the whole land belonged to me now—the Portland metro area. By the time I graduated from high school, I could get a stranger anywhere between a parameter marked by Vancouver, Washington; Tigard, Oregon; and Forest Grove, Oregon.

We always took the I-5 North back to Vancouver from Portland. We made this drive multiple times every week from church or from Grandma and Grandpa's house. On clear days, we observed the decapitated crater of Mount St. Helens looming over the community of Vancouver as we approached home.

The drives home boasted mountains beyond mountains. To the east there is Mount Hood looming with prominence, to the northeast Mount Adams barely peaking up over the ridge and on really clear, cloudless days, Mount Rainier flush behind St. Helens to the north. Many years later, I discovered another peak, so hidden that longtime Vancouver residents may not even know it can be seen. The very tip of Mount Jefferson slices through the hills to the south of Portland like a sharp prism, most noticeable during an orange-pink sunset.

These five peaks that define the farthest borders of my home country are just a small part of countless volcanoes that dot this side of the Pacific Ring of Fire and stand ever-unchanged in their snowcapped glory as single, solitary points of white. These were *my* mountains, and they represented stability. They lived at the farthest visible reaches, always appearing the same, week after week, ride after ride.

I'd not often been beyond these five great white peaks. They represented mystery and adventure. On the occasion when my family traveled beyond them, we found the adventure I was looking for. While everything close changed, the largest structures—those farthest away that I could not get to—remained the same.

─◆•◆•◆─

All, that is, except Mount St. Helens.

Growing up in the region, I heard the stories. Anyone who lived within one hundred miles of Mount St. Helens can tell you where they were on that day—May 18, 1980—and what they doing.

"It happened on a Sunday. We were driving to church, and we didn't know it had happened. We learned about the eruption once we got to church. When we came back home we could see the plume rise behind the Sylvan hills to the north."—My grandfather's account of the story as he watched it from Tigard, Oregon, about fifty miles away.

"Yakima was dark as midnight, and it was twelve o'clock in the afternoon. People's cars were so covered in ash you couldn't even see their license plate numbers."—A longtime Yakima, Washington resident whom I met in college while on a road trip.

"I was in college in Seattle. I'll never forget the day it blew. You could see smoke rising from the south."—Mom's fantastic account, like something out of Tolkien's *Lord of the Rings*.

"My mother, boy, did she hear it, she said, like a great loud shotgun, but I heard nothing, because we lived on the other side, the north side of a hill and the soundwaves just passed right over."—Robert Bussard, Bellingham, Washington, the other side of the state, 250 miles away.

I wanted to have my own story. I felt as if it were my own fault somehow, that I'd missed out on a major local event belonging to the history of my homeland. "Where were you, Jonathan, on the morning of May 18, 1980?... Oh, you're that young, huh? Why, I remember when the mountain erupted...I was on a solo flight three miles away from the action, and my port wing was struck by lightning. I parachuted to safety as my plane crashed into the spewing mouth of the volcano, exploding behind me like fireworks while I saved a baby eagle. You weren't even a twinkle in your father's eye then..."

I had no story.

—•◦•◦•—

But I do have a story...

Vancouver was my home. But when I went to college in Bellingham, on the other side of the state, my home, and everything I knew was gone... suddenly pulled out from under me.

I recall the move to Bellingham as a painful tearing of everything I loved from my heart where it lived deep inside. As we drove north, I looked out the window and watched each new landmark, each new building or bridge or land formation that I hadn't seen before get closer, and those I knew faded in the distance behind me. I was being divorced from the world as I had known it.

In September 2004, ten years after I first explored Ape Caves, I had to enter a new cave. It was the first few weeks of college, and I was living in an unfamiliar place, surrounded by unfamiliar people.

All of my friends and family—everyone I knew—were back home. So was my sense of belonging. My mountains were gone. My streets names, my bridges, my rivers and my radio towers were gone. No more biking with my best friend. No more memorable outdoor activities with my family. No more mystery hidden between the lives I lived stricken by a family split in two.

Bellingham and the surrounding county had plenty to offer. It had its own landmarks, its own street names and radio towers...even a bay that reminded me of the Columbia. It has its own volcano, Mount Baker, to the northeast...just like Mount St. Helens is to Vancouver. All of it was so similar to what I had known, but none of it was what I loved, and that made adapting harder.

A few weeks into school, I was talking to Mom one September afternoon in my yet-to-be-completely decorated dorm room, and she said those words: "Mount St. Helens is erupting again." And there it was. I couldn't believe it. All those years I waited, and two weeks after I left, I missed it. Again.

I exploded.

———◦•◦•◦———

I lived in a cave of gloom and pessimism that entire first year of college, only to emerge to a crowd of people happy to explore their new college existence. Some treated me like I was some scary creature hiding in the shadows of what I no longer had. On one unusually sunny day the next spring, a friend was visiting from home. We decided to make the drive to Artist Point at Mount Baker—my first drive up to the "new" mountain to get to know it. We drove along the winding two-lane highway into volcano country. As I passed the street names, and the houses, the trees, the rivers and the landmarks, the similarity of it all, each passing mile continued to be a source of sorrow.

The drive went on. After stopping at the ranger station outside of Glacier for a map, we began the windy ascent to the top of Mount Baker when I saw behind me the most incredible sight: Mount Shuksan loomed, sporting its jagged peak.

"What mountain is that?" I wondered. I never remember seeing it on any of my maps.

Jonathan's first view of Mount Shuksan.

Mount Shuksan from Artist Point in the winter of 2005.

It was an angel, menacing and magnificent. Its serrated, razor-sharp ridges were like those of no mountain I'd ever seen. Not like a dome-shaped volcano...more romantic. At the top of Shuksan is a peak shaped like a pyramid. I couldn't help but think of Jefferson, with its prism-like protrusion tearing through the fabric of the atmosphere.

Here was Shuksan, doing the same, and I felt the mystery...I felt adventure, waiting to be discovered in this new region. I couldn't stop staring at this wonderful sight, looking behind me while I was driving a steep cliff edge.

Then we arrived at the top of Artist Point, and there I found a universe of rippled ridges and craggy peaks as far as the eye could see. More than just the five peaks of my homeland, each isolated from one another, but rather hundreds of smaller, breathtaking snow-laden heads with their ancient earth-etched faces showing, all connected and lit up by a brazen sun. Mountains beyond mountains. There was no reason to be afraid.

Author Biographies

Stefeny Anderson was born and raised in Renton, Washington, and is a Washington girl through and through. After attending Seattle Pacific University and earning a degree in secondary education/social sciences, Stefeny headed out to the East Coast to seek a different life as a nanny. After four years there, she was drawn back to Renton. While back in the great state of Washington, she worked as a director at the YMCA, made a couple short movies and dreamed of writing the next great sitcom. This led to a short-lived migration to Los Angeles before she again moved back to the great city of Renton. She worked in event coordination and volunteered with an after-school program. She is now the educational director for an after-school arts program, CryOut!, for high school students. CryOut! offers students training in writing, music and visual arts.

Laura M. Gibson's essays and fiction have appeared in *Word Riot*, *Canteen* and the *Sun*, among other publications. She lives in the Pacific Northwest, where she works to start and sustain school gardens, and she blogs about writing, gardening and chicken wrangling at lauramgibson.com.

Gary R. Hafer is the John P. Graham Teaching Professor at Lycoming College in Williamsport, Pennsylvania. His short studies on writing instruction have appeared in *College English*, *The Journal of Developmental Education* and *Computers and Composition*. He is also production design editor for *Brilliant Corners*, a journal of jazz and literature. He is working on a book about teaching writing for professors outside the field of English.

Julie Hall grew up in Puyallup, Washington, and after roughly six years of school and traveling abroad, she moved back to the Pacific Northwest, where she and her family have put down their roots. She lives with her husband, daughter and son in Bellingham.

A former arts journalist, music researcher and novelist, **Patricia Herlevi** was born in Mount Vernon, grew up on Whidbey Island, attended Western Washington University and resided in Seattle for twenty-one years, where she honed her writing skills. She sells her novels, *Go Lucy* and *Agnes et Yves (Ma Vie en Bleu)*, on Create Space and Amazon. Her green fiction set in Washington State appears on Kindle as singles. Visit her at http:// pnwauthor.wordpress.com.

Kase Johnstun teaches written communications at Kansas State University. His work has appeared in numerous national and international publications, including *Creative Nonfiction*, the *Chronicle Review* and *Label Me Latina/o*. He is a regular contributor to the Good Men Project, and he is currently writing a creative nonfiction book about the epidemiology, medical history and lives affected by the birth defect craniosynostosis (McFarland, 2014).

Professor of English and director of creative writing at Lock Haven University, **Marjorie Maddox** has published *Perpendicular As I*; *Transplant, Transport, Transubstantiation*; *Weeknights at the Cathedral*; *When the Wood Clacks Out Your Name: Baseball Poems*; six chapbooks and over four hundred poems, stories and essays in journals and anthologies. She is the co-editor of *Common Wealth: Contemporary Poets on Pennsylvania*, author of two children's books from Boyds Mills Press and recipient of numerous awards, including Pushcart Prize nominations in both fiction and poetry. For more info and reviews, please see http://www.lhup.edu/mmaddoxh/biography.htm.

Lauren McKinney, an "Army brat," spent her childhood in Lawton, Oklahoma; Wayne, Pennsylvania; Schnenectady, New York; Augusta, Georgia; and two cities in Germany, Worms and Kaiserslautern. Her grandfathers were also both in the military, so Seattle, where her grandmother was raised, seemed like the closest thing to a hometown. Lauren has a PhD in English from Temple University and an MFA in creative nonfiction from Goucher College. She lives with her husband and two sons in Swarthmore, Pennsylvania, which she now considers her hometown.

Jonathan Metz grew up in Vancouver, Washington, and the neighboring Portland, Oregon area. He now lives in Bellingham, Washington, and is studying music composition and choral conducting. He is co-director of the EyeHear Music and Arts Collaboration and serves at First Baptist Church as director of worship and directs the FBC Sanctuary Choir. Also an avid poet, Jonathan has written over two hundred poems and has compiled a number of these poems into collections titled *The Baroque Linguistics, Our Clandestine Souls* and *Love, You*. He holds a bachelor of arts in music from Western Washington University.

Sue Kreke Rumbaugh's writing has appeared in the *Bicycle Review, Travel Writing Handbook, Pittsburgh Post Gazette* and the *Steubenville Herald-Star*. She has performed readings in western Pennsylvania and Carlow, Ireland. A native of Pittsburgh, Pennsylvania, Sue is an assistant professor of English at Carlow University, where she teaches creative writing courses including memoir, writing about place, craft and personal essay. She earned a bachelor of science degree in journalism (West Virginia University, 1979), master of public management (Carnegie Mellon University, 2000) and master of fine arts in creative writing (Carlow University, 2009). In addition to writing short pieces of creative nonfiction and fiction, she has a book-length memoir for which she is currently seeking a home and is working on a young adult book of fiction. When not sailing, playing tennis or traveling, Sue and her husband, Larry, reside in Glenshaw, Pennsylvania.

Cindy Sherwin, although born and raised in California, considers herself a faux-native of Washington. Moving to Bellingham in 1993, she embraced everything Northwest, including the rain. After a career in finance in the '80s, she stayed home for fifteen years to raise her three kids. Once they no longer needed her taxi services, she opened her own business, helping people plan for their long-term care needs.

With his wife and two children, **Matthew Taron** lives, teaches and sorts recyclables in Olympia, Washington. He enjoys walks in the rain, but not because they are romantic—just because he enjoys walking and lives in Olympia. He also appreciates a good sense of humor, but in a pinch, he knows how to make do with an average sense of humor and a couple of beers.

Sarah Eden Wallace is the author of *100 Years at the Northwest Washington Fair*. She first became familiar with the many fascinating stories of the fair during the nearly ten years she worked as an editor at the *Bellingham Herald*. A Phi Beta Kappa graduate of the University of Michigan, she had a summer job during college on a small dairy farm in Vermont. She was also an editor at *Phoenix Magazine*, the *Arizona Republic* and *Phoenix New Times*.

Stephen Weiser taught high school math and college English, worked for a Fortune 500 engineering and construction company, became a technical communications and marketing consultant and was most recently an emergency management bureaucrat. His fiction has appeared in *cold.drill*, the *North American Review* and *4 Minute Fictions*. He lives in Boise, Idaho.

About the Editors

Rebecca Beardsall works in the extended education department of Western Washington University. She also teaches in the English department at DeSales University. She grew up in Quakertown, Pennsylvania, and has lived in various places, including Scotland, Canada, Montana, New Zealand and Washington. She graduated with a BA in English from DeSales University and received her MA in English from Lehigh University. She has fifteen years' experience in freelance writing in the United States and abroad. Her poetry has been published in various literary journals.  She co-edited two books (September 2011) *Philadelphia Reflections: Stories from the Delaware to the Schuylkill* and *Western Pennsylvania Reflections: Stories from the Alleghenies to Lake Erie.*

Colleen Lutz Clemens is assistant professor of non-Western literatures at Kutztown University. Along with her poetry publications in *English Journal*, her essay in the anthology *Click* recounts her story of being her high school's first female tuba player. Her essay about her Pappy, who worked at Bethlehem Steel, was featured on public radio's "This I Believe" series. Most recently, her essay about her struggle to have a child was included in *TRIVIA*'s special issue on death and feminism. She is the author of several academic publications as well. She is co-editor of The History Press's *Philadelphia Reflections: Stories from the Delaware to the Schuylkill* and *Western Pennsylvania Reflections: Stories from the Alleghenies to Lake Erie*. She currently resides in Bucks County with her husband, their daughter and their two dogs.